بِسْمِ اللهِ الرَّحْمٰنِ الرَّحِيمِ

TOWARD THE ONE,
THE PERFECTION
OF LOVE, HARMONY, & BEAUTY,
THE ONLY BEING,
UNITED WITH ALL
THE ILLUMINATED SOULS
WHO FORM
THE EMBODIMENT OF
THE MASTER,
THE SPIRIT OF GUIDANCE

WE BEGIN IN THE NAME OF ALLAH
MOST MERCIFUL AND COMPASSIONATE

IN THE GARDEN

ALL RIGHT ALL RIGHT

...NOW LET'S DANCE

Samuel L. Lewis
(Sufi Ahmed Murad: Chisti)

Harmony Books   Lama Foundation
New York, New York   San Cristobal, New Mexico

COST DISTRIBUTION
15,000 copies

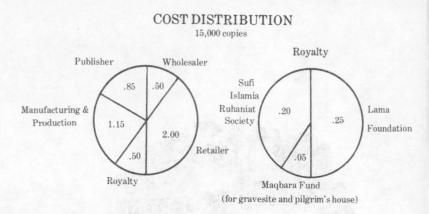

Royalty

Publisher   Wholesaler

.85   .50

Manufacturing & Production   1.15

2.00

.50

Royalty

Retailer

Sufi Islamia Ruhaniat Society   .20   .25   Lama Foundation

Royalty

.05

Maqbara Fund
(for gravesite and pilgrim's house)

Published by Harmony Books, a division of Crown Publishers, Inc., 419 Park Avenue South, New York, NY 10016.
Produced by the Lama Foundation, Box 444, San Cristobal, NM 87564.

Library of Congress Catalogue Card No. 75-27184
ISBN 0-517-524120
Manufactured by Modern Press, Albuquerque, New Mexico.

Many thanks to the following photographers: Mansur Johnson, Hiro Narita, William B. Giles, Jellaluddin Cave, Mouni, Rameshwar Dass, and other friends known and unknown.

The prayers "Saum", "Salat", "Khatum", and "Nayaz" were given by Pir-O-Murshid Hazrat Inayat Khan (1882-1927), as was the Invocation, "Toward the One".

"I feel like a gardener who planted a bunch of seeds and nothing came up; and again the next year he planted a bunch more seeds and nothing came up; and again the next year more seeds with the same result; and so on and on and on. And then this year, he planted a bunch of seeds: not only did they all come up, but all the seeds from the previous year came up and all the seeds from the year before, and so on. So I've just been frantically running around trying to harvest all the plants until Allah came to me and said, "Don't worry. Harvest what you can and leave the rest to Me."

Murshid Sam Lewis

TABLE OF CONTENTS

PREFACE 8
SUFI SAM by Ram Dass 10
A RIDDLE OF GOD by Pir Vilayat Khan 12
"FOR REAL" by Joe Miller 14
GROWING IN HIS GARDEN — Experiences
   with Murshid Sam 17
THE GARDENER: LIFE AND TIMES 47
FAMILY ALBUM 61
SAUM (prayer) 74
SPIRITUAL ARCHITECTURE 75
HOUSE OF TANSEN (poem) 88
BOOK OF HEART (poem) 89
SPIRITUAL PRACTICES:
   INTRODUCTION 95
   WALK 98
   DIVINE ATTRIBUTES WALKS 112
   DANCE 122
   BREATH 136
   MEDITATION 148
GATHAS OF THE DHARMA 157
KARUNA YOGA GITA 173
SUFI VISION AND INITIATION 207
DATES: FROM THE DIARIES 221
BOOK OF COSMIC PROPHECY (selections) 243
AFTERWORD by Dusty Roads..................... 273
GOD CALLS (poem) 278
GLOSSARY 281
BIBLIOGRAPHY and PUBLISHED WORKS 286
KHATUM (prayer) 288

PREFACE

Murshid Sam frequently quoted Al-Ghazali (known as the "proof of Islam"): "Sufism is based on experiences not premises."

Murshid was a Teacher before he was a writer, a Prophet before a poet, a Master before a commentator. His writings show that he lived and spoke from a number of planes. He could invoke the muse, and he could also efface into the Prophet Samuel. Except for his early poetry (including "To Me Hath Been Granted a Garden"), he wrote to communicate the Presence of God, not to create works of art. He always spoke and wrote with distinctive authority and devotion, and therein lies his art.

"My work in this world and the next is not writing 'Cookbooks for the Astral Plane.' I am all for that. I am all for that in a manner far from sarcasm as I am for motherhood. My functions do not include writing 'Cookbooks for the Astral Plane' or being a mother. My work at the lowest levels includes leading – and I mean leading – people to rise above the distinctions and differences which divide men . . ."

(in a letter to Lama, February 11, 1970)

His universalism derived from his esoteric training in the Far East, the Middle East, and in this country. He loved to quote Whitman: "In all people I see myself." Sam taught people, not "isms."

He taught through his being, spontaneously and directly, as a Zen master for sure. He taught through his mantric (prayerful) dances, as a dervish and a bhakta (a "lover" in the Hindu terminology). And he also spoke to people's intellects, for he was knowledgeable in the scriptures of all the world's religions.

Sam went unheeded through most of his life . . . "a voice crying in the wilderness . . ." until the "hip" generation began coming of age in his native San Francisco. He knew himself to

8

be a *"Pied Piper"* but he never asked to be made a hero or a demi-god. He staked his reputation on his students, so we thought it appropriate to begin with their descriptions of experiences with Sam.

Murshid came and taught at Lama on two occasions and chose to be buried here. The book was edited and laid-out at Lama and naturally reflects some of the perspective of this place. When teaching here, Murshid spent several hours daily in the garden. (His centers in California were named Mentorgarden, Garden of Inayat, and Garden of Allah.) As is explained in The Book of Cosmic Prophecy, *he was working in the spiritual garden as well as in the physical.*

Great assistance in this book came from a number of editors from the Sufi Order in San Francisco and Tucson, most notably MaSheikh Wali Ali Meyer, who, as Murshid's last (over-worked) secretary, organized fifty years of writings into three huge filing cabinets. Thanks also go out to the editors of Harmony Books, New York, who came so far to help us prepare the book for the general public.

Our hope is that this volume may serve to introduce you to the vast work of Murshid Sufi Sam, and our prayer is that his words may serve to bring you closer to God.

Lama Foundation
August, 1975

"I'm quite willing to work here as a flunky, and pull weeds, or do anything of the kind. But when it comes to the dancing class, then I'm the Master, not in anything else."

−S.A.M. at Lama

9

SUFI SAM

by Ram Dass

The last time Sufi Sam and I met was in 1970 in Central Park in New York City. A movie was being filmed of me in a variety of scenes: chanting with tamboura at dawn by the duck pond; talking to people at the zoo; on 5th Ave., with Pir Vilayat, and in darshan at Rudi's ashram. In mid-afternoon the schedule called for a sequence of Sufi dance with Murshid in the park. As usual I felt some trepidation.

Initially there were perhaps twenty dancers present in the sheep meadow. But Sam slowly drew in onlookers. The dance was done to the chant of OM SHRI RAM JAI RAM JAI JAI RAM with Sam giving separate signals to the women and to the men as to who would sing and in what direction to move. This particular mantra, though chanted slightly differently, was the one that was continuously chanted in the small temple in the foothills of the Himalayas where I was with my Guru. Suddenly through the chant Murshid and I met in an entirely new space — one of profound antiquity as spiritual brothers. Not only as fellow Jews who had absorbed from the East. For that was but this lifetime. No, the recognition was of a connection which

10

transcended time and space — reaching back even to the One from which all becomes manifest.

Of course that recognition lasted only briefly but it put into perspective all the other feelings which were, of course, there too: the ego discomfort, paranoia, etc. Over time the confusion of that moment has given way to the understanding that to truly know the Living Spirit you *must* acknowledge the insanity. There must be balance between God consciousness and world consciousness. You must look down as well as up . . . lest you trip!

Murshid, like Gurdjieff, Don Juan, the Tibetans Marpa, Tilopa, Milarepa, my own Guru, Neem Karolli Baba, and many others, represents the true tantric teachings. Such teachings transcend the rule book and are exquisitely appropriate to the immediate situation. Each teaching reflects the balance of merciful compassion, humor, love, and the steely blade of the discriminative sword of caring that awakens beings to Truth. Such a teacher uses the materials at hand — both materially and psychologically to supportively rouse the sleeping seeker to that which is beyond illusion.

But who then is such a teacher? For each seeker who comes in contact with such a person knows him or her in a different way — seeing mirrored only his or her own projections. The answer is that such a being, through the true surrender into the Will of God, the Tao, the Buddha mind, the Divine Mother, *is* the teaching . . . *is* the Living Spirit made manifest.

Long Live Murshid Sam!

PIED PIPER OF GOD
by Pir Vilayat Khan

"Vilayat came to one of our regular meetings and was amazed at our work in music and dancing. Sam introduced him: 'I am not going to talk. This would take time away from the visiting speaker. Besides I want to cry.'"

Diaries –May, 1968

Murshid Sam, Sufi Ahmed Murad, was an endearing, buoyant riddle of God. I suppose he left it to you whether you let him lead you into that riddle, or grasped his way out. He was obviously trying to point out to you a way you did not know.

He had the art of conjuring enthusiasm into the luke-warm and faint-hearted, crashing through traffic jams into wide open spaces, and showing people where they were before they knew they were there.

His joy was contagious, winning, devastating, and earmarked him as the Pied Piper of the new age, luring happy and not so happy people into new dimensions of being high. He could bring down a house by the punch of his opinion and build another one somewhere else.

Never a dull moment in his writings, where he would sometimes touch a chord that set untold vibrations into resonance. But he came through into one's life still stronger just in his being, for he would never fail to bring the human touch within sight while being in the throes of a mystical mood.

'Why not do something rather than talk about it?' was his motto. If you wish to do something about joy and ecstasy, you will dance the dance of Shiva, and the world will dance with you. And so, out of the traditional dervish whirl, emerged the dance of the happy people, and in no time it spread through the states and beyond the seas to Europe.

As the energy rose and blossomed and spread, it cross-bred with other streams and currents. The seed of the Message of the New Age began to re-emerge above the frozen earth of wintertide into the spring of renewal and these seeds continue to flourish in the gardens of the world.

"FOR REAL"

by Joe Miller

Sam planted a lot of seeds, and he's had a lot of marvelous results. The work in Jerusalem, the Sufi choir, this book, were all started by a little guy, about whom if you had seen him on the street you would have said, "I don't know exactly what to make of this guy. He's a crackpot or fanatic or he's nuts." Actually he was a combination of all three, because in Sufism he'd be called a Madzub. Madzubs will not conform to any particular pattern, and will continue to be eclectic in what they *give* to people and what they put out to help people live. And Sam was such a person.

He struck a note that was not Sufism from some other land, but Sufism became the flavor of the good earth here in United States itself. It's an important thing. The important thing is that it's the flavor of what the *people* are here, what they'll put up with, what they won't put up with. And it's honest, straight-forward, and if it was necessary to kick 'em and push 'em around, he'd kick 'em and push 'em around. But he was for real.

I can remember when I would meet him occasionally, maybe he was in such a hurry to do something for his kids (disciples) that he had about a third of his face shaved and maybe on the other side he made one swipe with the safety razor and he'd come down the street with his thick glasses on, looking like a little Beatle or something. But Heart? WOW — the joint was *filled* with Heart. He *helped* people.

I remember Sam came to the Theosophical Society one day, and he was gonna do one of his new dances, see he was gonna do a fancy dance. The lady who was running the society at that time said, "You know I didn't know if I'd better let dear Sam do the dance or not, because I was afraid he was gonna lose his pants." Sam didn't care what he lost or when he lost it, as long as he was pushing the fact of love, harmony and beauty.

He was a true Sufi. I don't care what they think. The other thing I would like to have you understand about "Sufi" is that Sufis don't have to use exactly the same pattern. There is nothing of a dogma or creed connected with genuine Sufism. The Murshids and the Pirs enlighten their pupils, and when they expand and learn from heart to heart and start Living it, then each one of them may have a different way to give out this Message of the Heart which is always there. This "baraka" (if you will), which is called Grace in most of our Christian works, is the important thing.

I was going to tell you more about Sam. Sam could be depended upon always, and depended to explode if you got idiotic in your performance of what you were learning from him. I can remember in that movie Sunseed, Sam was in, one of the most important things that he conveyed in the whole picture was when he was playing solitaire sitting at the table, and the kid that interviewed him said, "Well you know, you get different conceptions about things." And all Sam had said was "Yeah, that's the trouble: Concepts!" and kept on playing solitaire.

In another part of the picture someone asked, "What would you be happy about if you were going to leave this life?" And he said, "If just two or three of my disciples Got It and started Living It." So this person asked, "Well, how would you know?" He says, "You couldn't help but know because they would shine." Isn't that beautiful? It's so simple and right to the point.

He was a down to earth person. He wouldn't give you any fancy trip on a nice pink cloud. No, rather than do that, he would kick you and say, Now what's the matter with you? Come off your high horse and look at things the way they really are. See things around you as they are. And realize your at-one-ment with the One. And radiate love to everybody. But no hooks on that love. Nothing taken back. Just let it flow out.

The thing is that it's so wonderful and so simple, the work that the Sufis do, that other people won't believe it. You see, there's nothing to enslave you. You don't need to spend the next twenty years of your life contemplating your navel til it gets as big as a washtub, or facing a wall and trying to go blank. Nothing like that, just Love.

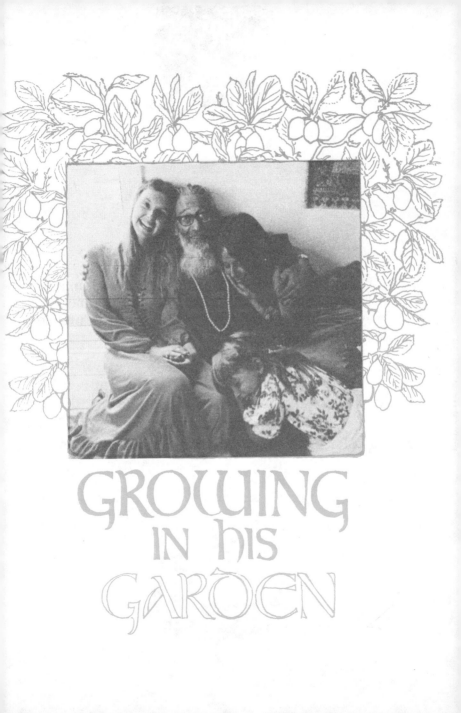

GROWING
IN HIS
GARDEN

These are stories told by members of Lama as well as disciples in Sam's native San Francisco. They serve to introduce Murshid and his unique style of Spiritual teaching.

"People ask why don't I do more for Buddhism. My tomato experiments have succeeded beyond expectations. My fertilizer experiments have brought excellent results. The people around the greenhouse are so harmonious and cooperative all around . . ."

CROWING IN HIS GARDEN-EXPERIENCES WITH MURSHID

One disciple offered this description of his initiation by Murshid Sam:

"As I approached the Mentorgarden (Murshid's center) my stomach started to flip flop and I got cold chills, along with the shakes. As I entered the hall I felt something missing, for there were not any trumpets, nor even any music. Wali Ali, his secretary, came in and asked me what I wanted. To my own surprise I explained that I had come to receive *bayat* (initiation). He said to wait a minute, because Murshid was taking a nap, and he would have to wake him. I told myself that this surely couldn't be true: Murshid napping before an initiation? He was probably meditating in order to contact the Hierarchy. Somewhat perplexed, I waited until Murshid walked into the room, or I should say sleep-walked into the room. He was attired in a v-necked t-shirt, a pair of stained khaki pants, one sock on and one sock half off. He asked my purpose in coming and I explained. Upon hearing this, he called Wali Ali and began immediately. I felt like saying, "But where is the incense, the music, the robes?", but totally annihilated, I stood there. Murshid was about three-fourths through when he told me to drink from this cup. But there wasn't a cup! He asked Wali Ali to get one while we waited. Wali Ali was right back with the cup, but there wasn't anything in it. Murshid said it was all right, just fake it and act as if you're drinking from it. When the initiation was over he asked me if I wanted to watch Perry Mason with him while he peeled potatoes. Stunned, I could only say yes. During Perry Mason all he did was peel potatoes and give me penetrating glances out of the corner of his eye. When this was over I got up and left, somewhat dismayed. After a time I realized that this was the most paramount of experiences in my life.

Fazul

Murshid Sam had a gruff exterior, which was easily seen through by those who were to become his disciples and which successfully put off the merely curious and those who were destined to follow a different path. With those who became his followers he was frank and totally unpretentious, and often embarrassingly spontaneous. The half-hearted could only cringe at some of his behavior, while his "lovers" received the highest teachings from his mundane actions:

Moineddin and I used to hitchhike to the Mentorgarden every Sunday to 'help' Murshid. The first time I helped prepare lunch I wasn't familiar with Murshid's cooking style yet. After he had

20

boiled some vegetables in lots of water I drained them into the sink. Just then he walked in and shouted, 'We never throw vegetable water away!' Although I had poured it into the dirty dish water, he poured it all into the soup.

Fatima

It was his example that was the teaching. One time walking back from the grocery store I said to him, "Murshid, I would rather go in shopping with you than hear you lecture." It says in the teachings that a mystic is one who can do without doing and say without speaking. What could he have taught me that day? Concentration, as he walked in search of some cranapple juice? Friendliness, as he spoke to the checker? Positivity, as he led me across the street? Silence, as he walked in the presence of God?

Mansur

After a night's sleep, which was often filled with visions of dances and practices for his disciples, he would leap into the day with alarming energy. After performing his prayers alone, he could be a stand-up comedian at breakfast, a relentless letter-writer during the morning, a generous host and friend at noon, an enthusiastic gardener in the afternoon, an advisor and brilliant lecturer in the evening, and Master of the Dance any time at all. His active interest in actually feeding people led him on many journeys to seed producers, soil scientists, greenhouse experts and ecologists in California, the Middle East and Asia. Experiments with California cherry trees which Murshid recommended for the Holy Land are being carried out now. Friends and followers are beginning to implement Sam's plans for other projects in water desalination, soil reclamation, and deep drilling for water (which may mean more attention to "unsuccessful" oil drills).

Editor

MARIJUANA VS. TOMATOES

When I interviewed him on film on the subject of marijuana he said he was neither for nor against. I think this was wise. Afterwards, he said, "Tomatoes." He explained that some years before tomatoes were believed to have intoxicating qualities. That's why they were known as "love apples."

Mansur

FOLLOW YOUR NOSE

I have written to the magazine *Sufi Speaks* an unpublished letter, in which I relate my first meeting with Murshid. I thought he had a big nose, I wrote. Fatima and Moineddin wrote me about him. They told me that he taught walking and breathing, and that they believed he could take them the fastest to where they wanted to go. Shortly after I arrived in San Francisco, he taught me to walk up the steepest hills without any fatigue.* I noticed his nose because he was a master of breath.

Mansur

* see Spiritual Practices Section

MY BEST FRIEND

From the very first time I walked in on the 4th of July, I never left. I don't know why I stayed. Nothing unusual happened. But he told me about his credentials and I was impressed. It must have been his tremendous self-confidence. Anyone that self-confident must know something. He was nothing special, just my best friend, someone I miss now, the one to whom I must give credit for anything good or true or beautiful that I do, the one from whom I must hide if I do wrong.

Murshid had warned: "There is a great danger, without there being a danger at all, of overestimating a Murshid and finding also a very human being."

Mansur

HERE COMES THE NURSE

Inayat Khan has written, "Consideration is the sign of the wise." When I went to see Murshid in the hospital on January 7th, 1971, it was clear to me that he didn't need any food. He was so strong, his atmosphere was so magnificent, I felt it would be a shame to interrupt his retreat with a meal. When those present suggested it was meal time and that he should eat, I took a little piece of fruit cocktail and held it in my fingers and held my fingers up to his mouth and he licked some of the juice off the fruit. I knew this was very nourishing and enjoyable to him. Nevertheless those present were not satisfied even when I ate some more of his meal so as to make it appear that he had nibbled a little. A large nurse soon appeared. She had one goal, to make him eat. He did. When I left he was sitting up chewing. He left the body ten days later. Even so, he was so kind and considerate of the nurse as to eat when he didn't want to.

Mansur

"I think he was born to — born in the feel of the old prophets. And I don't think his family or many people appreciated what he was or what he was doing."

Paul Reps

GARDEN CUISINE

Murshid used to cook breakfast at the *Khankah* in Novato every Sunday. Usually he made what he called a "fritata." It consisted of garden vegetables, leftovers, eggs and flour baked in the oven. The vegetables which he grew were swished through a bowl of water, boiled and added to the rest. Every Sunday I looked forward to finding rocks, dirt, snails, earwigs and aphids in my portion.

Fatima

"The only two things I don't allow in my house are empty stomachs and cold feet."

S.A.M.

MEDITATION

A Murshid meditation in class rarely lasted more than one minute at the longest. He said if you didn't get it right away, don't force it.

Fatima

TWO NAPS

A. I looked out the back door of the *Khankah* and was startled to see Murshid lying face down in the middle of the main path to the back gate. I thought he had collapsed. When I went to check, he was peacefully snoring — just taking an afternoon snooze.

B. Moineddin saw him sleeping under the oak tree. When he arose, Moineddin thought he'd take a nap in the exact spot and get Murshid's *baraka* (blessing). When he lay down he found he was on rocks and oak apples and bumps — on totally uncomfortable ground.

Fatima

HOW I GOT MY NAME

Receiving a spiritual name is supposed to be a very sacred and meaningful event. I received mine in my garden in Bolinas while weeding with Murshid. He cried, "I've got it!

"Got what?"

"Your spiritual name. First I went from Pat (my old name) to fat (I was) and then came Fatima."

Fatima

"Never argue with a pregnant lady because she is always right."

S.A.M.

When I entered Murshid's office at the *Khankah* for my first interview, he asked:

"What can I do for you?"

"Well, I have no questions," I said, "I just felt I was supposed to come and see you."

"Well, thank you for coming," he replied, and walked out the door.

Shabda

FAULTS SCHMAULTS

One day when he was feeling his own faults very strongly, Murshid went into meditation and asked God what to do. He received the answer:

"Your faults are My Perfections."

Shabda

ASPARAGUS OUR BUGS

Murshid's love for his disciples often manifested in very concrete ways. Once I told him that we had aphids in our garden.

"Follow me," he said. He led me into the kitchen and grabbed up a sack of asparagus.

"Take these. They were left over from last night's meal. Spray the plants with them and come back with the results."

It worked.

Shabda

When I first met Murshid I was depleted physically, mentally, and emotionally. I had neither love, nor joy, nor peace, nor health. The first thing Murshid said to me was "Sit up straight! There is nothing you have ever done in your life that was wrong!"

At my second interview, Murshid had me sit in a chair opposite him. He told me to look into his eyes and asked me if they frightened me. I replied "No." I looked into his eyes for three or four minutes. With eyes like swords of lights, Murshid cut through and completely released me from pain, fear, defeat, hopelessness and self-pity. Then he said "God bless you," and embraced me. The interview was over.

Zeinob

Murshid often said to his disciples, "If you don't have the dishes done, don't bother coming to meetings."

Zeinob

WIPED OUT

There was an incident that occurred in 1968, when I'd already been totally shattered by psychedelics. Somebody slipped me some mescalin and belladonna on the sly. I couldn't sleep, I was really wrecked, so I rushed over to Murshid.

"What's the matter," he asked.

I told him what had happened and said I thought I

was going crazy. He sat me down in a chair, with the explanation,

"You have to sit down in a chair because you're too tall."

Then he put his arms around me and held me like a baby. He just breathed and created an aura of protection around me. After about twenty minutes he asked,

"You feel better?" Then he repeated about three times, "I don't normally do this."

Vashishta

In the middle of the dancing one Sunday, Murshid suddenly stopped and asked, "Where's Hassan?"

Somebody said, "He's got a really high fever and doesn't feel well. He's upstairs in bed."

Murshid looked at me. I stopped dancing and ran upstairs where I found Hassan asleep on the bed, very feverish. For some reason, instead of putting my hands on him, I sat down about three feet away and started pouring energy through my fingertips and eyes at him.

Then all of a sudden I felt an incredible rush of energy coming through me and out my hands and fingers and my back felt like a lightning bolt. I turned around to see Murshid standing behind me in the doorway, pointing his hands at me pointing my hands at Hassan on the bed. Hassan recovered immediately. It blew me out.

Saul

ARRIVAL AT LAMA

Our first "teacher" was coming to Lama. I entered a door into the Albuquerque Airport and before I had taken ten steps, a little man with stringy hair, beard, an ill-fitting gray suit and huge-lensed glasses peered up at me and said very loud and very fast, "I-know-all- the-secrets-of-the-cosmos, there-isn't-any- level-on-which-I-haven't-been, and-I-can- answer-any-question-you-might-have . . ." and he went on non-stop for four hours; the whole three hour drive to the Lama Foundation and then the invasion of the nightly meeting for an incredible monologue in which it was clear that he was unique, outrageous and very, very funny. After five years I have come to believe that his opening statement was simple reporting as he arrived for duty. I think his duty was (is) as an enlistment officer. In spite of my almost total disapproval of his style, I realized from the beginning I was following his direction about the planet, and the example of personal freedom which he demonstrated.

Asha

FISHY

Murshid didn't fool around. He arrived at Lama with two gallons of fish emulsion and he kept it under his bed when he wasn't spraying it.

Asha

29

PRASAD

One day soon after his arrival he announced that
he was going to give *darshan* (interview; literally:
'vision'), and I was to sit next to him and record the
event. He collected some Chinese cabbages from the
garden and had them heaped to his left on the table.
He had someone outside escorting the members of
the community and the stray Sunday visitors in one
by one. Someone would come in and sit down and he
would ask their name and age and make a remark:
"you don't *have* to get it through sex," "treat your
child as though it is the Divine Infant who is in your
care," after which he would look at me and tell me to
write down next to the name "B," "R," or "K" (and
then he would flex and stare with his glasses off for
about a minute and dismiss that person, giving them
a long hunk of wilted Chinese cabbage. "Prasad," he
would say.) When it was my turn, he asked me,
"Whose darshan do you want?" I asked what choice
I had. He said, "Buddha, Ram, or Christ," (he made
Christ "K" for Krishna) and then he decided on "K"
for me and gave me the stare . . . which I received,
got my cabbage, and closed the record book.

Asha

30

PERFECT MARRIAGE

I once asked Murshid if he had ever known a good marriage.

He said, "Only one. They were Indian and he spent six months of every year in Paris."

Asha

Once I was forced to stay home and wash the "family" dishes and miss the first half of one of Murshid's meetings. I arrived in a bit of a huff. Murshid immediately sidled up to me and chanted:

"Give a little, get a little, give a little, get a little, give a little, get a little."

Khabira

KRISHNA'S GLANCE

Do you know what it is like to be looked at by Krishna? You either want to run away in total embarrassment, or risk everything and give back the glance. It had nothing to do with age or appearance; it was a glance. I would have followed him anywhere, but he didn't ask that.

Sahaida

NURSERY SCHOOL

When he was at San Francisco City College, he worked in the nursery experimenting in the flats. He was deeply interested in seeds, in grasses and grains that could be used to feed Asia. He worked with seed catalog people in our country and contacted some of the heads of these research firms so that our hybrid grains and crops could be used with the simple plowing and irrigation methods of those (Asian) countries. Few listened. Also at that time he was present and active in the first session of the United Nations in San Francisco. As he grew older he was deeply interested in mostly what they were doing for Asian people — or, rather, what they were *not* doing for the Asian people. And he foresaw the Vietnam debacle with the French and the great starvation that would hit the lower classes, and he was hopefully working to prevent that type of starvation, mass starvation and migration we are seeing today.

Murshida Vera Corda

ATLAS

I saw the states that he went through and I saw him like Atlas carrying the great world on his shoulders, bent over, just previous to the time of the flower children. Then I would see him on the streets in the Civic Center near the library and call out to him and couldn't catch up with him because a bus would come between us or something would stop me physically, and he would be gone. I couldn't catch him; he had turned a corner or gone into a building. He was out of sight. And time and again I'd be so upset, for I was so close to him, yet couldn't touch him. But I would always see that image, the bent-over shoulders, the old gray tweed overcoat, and this big aura filled with the world he was carrying on his shoulders.

Murshida Vera

Samuel was not an ordinary human being, and anyone who tried to approach him that way started off on the wrong foot, because he could be Yiddish, pushy, insulting, overegotized. One could find him a man who was going to plow through, whether you like it or not. But if you met him and looked at him in the Spirit, then you would understand that here was a man who had a divine work to do and no obstacle or life situation could stop him.

Murshida Vera

MR. NATURAL

In the 1930's he lived so much in the spiritual body that if someone hadn't taken care of him he would have forgotten to take a bath, change his clothes or put on a sweater. He was totally immersed in the Inner world . . . I could tell you some incidents of this forgetfulness of the physical body which were hilarious when we were young, and sometimes embarrassing too, to those of the older generation. They would sometimes quote Murshid Inayat Ḳhan, who always wore his slippers, who always had his robe on, who always combed his beard and his hair. And here was Samuel, without a robe, unkempt and unmindful of the body.

Murshida Vera

SPIRIT BODY

The night he fell down the steps I felt a tremendous pain, and my conscious mind said, "This is impossible!" I denied it, and immediately the manifestation in the physical body went into the spiritual body, into Light; and I knew that he stood before me in the spirit body. He communicated with that image of light and then disappeared, and then the feeling of ice came slowly down through each center of my body, and I thought, "What has happened to Samuel?" I immediately got up and got my address book and called this number and asked, "What has happened to Samuel?"

Many times in real life Sam had come to my house. He would just come. He'd just appear at the door unexpectedly. It would usually be at a time when I was in trouble, when I needed him for some reason. The minute I began saying in my mind, "This can't be; this is not possible," then of course he went into the light and disappeared. This time I realized that he had come to inform me and to bid his farewell. I felt his blessing very strongly. I felt an enfoldment which I had often felt before. Many times when I sat before him I would see my own aura, which is a rare thing. I would see my own aura — the fingers of my aura out like this, you know. And I would see his aura always hooded like the cobra, and his hood would come out and envelop my head, and mine would go out and envelop his shoulders. And there would be a tremendous feeling in every center of my body, like a fluttering, a feeling of fluttering wings and then a warm slow vibration would envelop me. And Murshid has always come that way since his passing.

Murshida Vera Corda
in a taped interview

A WALKING, KNOCKING ENCYCLOPEDIA

The astrologer Gavin Arthur used to say that Sam had more knowledge than the encyclopedia. When he used to live in the room next to him in San Francisco's Japan town, Gavin would knock on the wall and ask him questions. He said Murshid was quicker and more accurate than the Encyclopedia Brittanica which he also had.

Wali Ali

Murshid once said: "I refuse to make the same mistakes Inayat Khan made; I would rather make my own new mistakes."

Wali Ali

MY SECRET

He was so many different people, acting whatever way he deemed proper to fulfill the functions needed by the particular situation which he faced. *"My secret is controlled schizophrenia"* he once said.

Wali Ali

In 1970 Moineddin, the man whom Murshid appointed as his spiritual successor, became ill and went to the hospital. It was a problem of excessive water retention in his system and his condition progressively deteriorated until the doctors frankly considered him on the point of death, with very little hope of recovery. All this time Murshid refused to go to see him in the hospital. He would talk to me about it. "I've got work to do." But still Moineddin got worse and worse and Murshid was getting ready to leave for New York City on a trip on behalf of Hallelujah the Three Rings, so he agreed to go to the hospital because he didn't want him to die while he was gone. "I'm going to give him hell."

He later reported it to me. "I didn't give him a breath. I told him he might think he was going to slip off into heaven but he was sadly mistaken, he was going straight to hell, until he could come back and fulfill his purpose. If he wanted to lie on his back all the time he could get a job as a mattress tester. And then I left." Murshid told me to go in and give him another positive treatment while he was gone, which I did by cheerfully and emphatically telling him all the activities that were going on and then leaving immediately. After Murshid's visit, Moineddin immediately began to get better. He returned from the hospital shortly before Murshid's own death.

To quote from Murshid's description of Fudo, (the Protector of the Dharma), "Fudo is the wise guide who does not confuse sentimentality with love."

Wali Ali

A CARD

He would often play solitaire while he dictated a letter or even while interviewing someone (as shown in the movie *Sunseed*). It helped him keep his mind from jumping; he used it as a positive concentration. And he would often turn to me in the course of a day and say, "The cards are coming up very good (or bad)." I later learned that he was reading the whole external world as signs from the manifest God. Even more he used to read the reactions which people and situations had to him personally and which he saw as significant on a world level. Everything had become a source of continuous revelation, and his inner and outer life was seen as a reflection of the globe in the mirror of his heart.

Wali Ali

MURSHID WHO?

Whenever I spoke up he listened; he listened for the ring of truth; he listened as if it was God Himself speaking; it could be a most disconcerting experience. I came to understand that that blanket of his energy field was like a test for those around him to be able to master a certain amount of positivity in order to break through. Thus one found after his passing that his disciples had been transformed into very positive beings, capable of taking the initiative in the same fashion as their Murshid.

Wali Ali

HOSPITAL FARE

Prior to Murshid's death, he was in a hospital in what appeared to be a state of semi-consciousness. Although the hospital staff may have viewed him as being in a totally "irrational" or "incoherent" state, a number of his disciples experienced his ability to return from another plane, at will, to communicate with his characteristic strength and lucidity. When his secretary walked in, for example, he immediately emerged from the "coma" and dictated a letter to his Murshid in Pakistan.

As I walked up to his bed, to spend the afternoon sitting with him, his eyes lit up with joyful recognition and my being was flooded with ecstasy — which lasted perhaps only a few seconds of worldly time. During the afternoon Murshid tossed and turned almost continuously. A rash on his body and certain bodily disfunctions caused him great discomfort, although on the day that I visited him his physical pain seemed to be on the periphery of his consciousness and not at all central to it. The area around his bed was flooded with radiance.

Murshid had been muttering unintelligibly. He began to try to reach through the bars of the hospital bed. I was sitting next to the bed and there was a table there with a small carton of milk on it. I knew that Murshid hadn't eaten anything that day and I thought that he might be hungry. "What do you want, Murshid? Do you want something?" I asked him. The only reply was the mysterious mumbling, until I tried to give him the milk. He said, vociferously, "No!" Yet he kept trying to reach something with his hands, and so I asked repeatedly "Do you want something, Murshid?" Suddenly he yelled, and I mean yelled, "Yes!" Astonished, I asked "What, what do you want?" "YOU!" he roared, and reaching his arms up like a child, he pulled my head down over the bars of the bed (I thought I might fall in head first) and gave me one of those inimitable Murshid kisses — a grinning smack on the lips. We remained in a state of delight, itches and pain and coma notwithstanding, for the rest of the afternoon. Murshid left his body a day or so later.

Mouni

LEWIS AND SULLIVAN

Shortly after I became an initiate, I had an appointment with Murshid to receive my spiritual practices. It happened to be my birthday and I didn't know that Murshid made a big deal about birthdays. He took me to dinner at an Indonesian restaurant. Then we went to hear Gilbert and Sullivan's "Iolanthe", all about fairies and other dancing things. We sat in the balcony, and Murshid sang out loudly along with the chorus. All around us people started going, "Shhh! Shhh!". Murshid appeared not to hear them; he was totally lost in the music. Finally a man came over and tapped him on the shoulder. Murshid leaned back in his chair quiet but disappointed. After that, nothing that Murshid did could ever embarrass me.

Ahura (Shirin)

YOU ARE THE MURSHID

I was having an ego dispute with my pottery partner which was not readily resolving itself. I went to Murshid and asked what to do. Gruffly, he said, "I don't care what you do, just remember, *You* are Murshid! *You* are Murshid!" I went away satisfied and filled with confidence that I was right. Immediately the dispute ceased to exist.

I forgot all about the incident. Four years later I was driving to L.A. with a fellow disciple, reminiscing about Murshid. "Do you know Murshid once told a story about you when he was in New York?" "No, tell me," I said.

"Two of my disciples were fighting and came to me wanting my support. Well, I fixed that one! I told them both, '*You* are Murshid!'"

Ahura (Shirin)

Murshid said at a Monday meeting: "There are some who worship the Divine Mother and others who become the Divine Mother."

Moineddin

VISITING HOURS

On the most unbearable night of pain in Novato General Hospital (summer, 1970) the doctor gave me a shot of morphine. During the middle of that night I had a vision of Murshid. He was in the captaincy of a whole army of saints and masters, a legion of known and unknown beings. They were all

chanting in unison, but Murshid's voice was loudest
and also tenderest.

Moineddin

GOD IS EVERYWHERE

I remember the smell of the incense Murshid used
to burn when we went to his meetings at
Clementina Street. You couldn't separate it from
anything, from Murshid, his speech, the people who
sought his guidance, anything. Even the bathroom
down the hall was like a shrine.

The whole life was a sacred mystery, pervaded by
devotion, and we drank from the cup of a love
greater than giving or receiving. Now that cup is
broken, but the love which shatters and heals,
continues to flow.

Moineddin

The first recollection I have of more than a "hello"
from Sufi Sam was at the back of the Avalon
Ballroom. That evening Allen Ginsberg and Swami
Bhaktivedanta were leading Hare Krisna chanting.
It was at the height of the Haight-Ashbury promise.
Sam, whom I didn't recognize, was sitting at an
empty table, looking a bit like a chaperone at a high
school dance. Because of my age I felt that way a bit
too, and so I sat down next to him. He started a
monologue concerning the evening, his community,
compliments about my work with Tim Leary,
Korea, food. The topics he covered extended far
beyond those that I can recall. Rather than listening
to him, I was experiencing the uneasy feeling that
this peculiar fellow was "putting me on." My ego

was on guard. He was obviously mad as a hatter . . . and yet . . . not quite.

In truth I felt that uneasy guarded feeling every time we met. (Neil Cassady used to make me feel much the same way.) Always mixed liberally into his non-stop deliveries were numbers of statements that seemed to be so blatantly paranoid, that I kept finding the psychologist in me coming forth in its benevolently patronizing aspect.

But in addition to the confusion of bumbly, flattered, benevolent, patronizing and guarded feelings that Sam evoked in me that first evening, I found a genuine love for this man, whose love poured out of him as he spoke on and on that evening, many of his words lost in the sounds of the ocean of Hare Krisna! Hare Krisna! Krisna! Krisna! Hare! Hare! Hare Rama! Hare Rama! Rama! Rama! Hare! Hare!

We met several more times — now in the panhandle of Golden Gate Park, now at a restaurant, now at a meeting. Our visits were too few, for my ego made it difficult for me to go out of my way to seek that bitter-sweet relationship even though I knew in my heart that Sufi Sam represented an honest and genuine connection to the Living Spirit.

Baba Ram Dass

"AS LITTLE CHILDREN"

The first lesson of *Tassawuri* that Murshid Sam taught me occurred when I observed him walking up the path between the dance dome and the kitchen. Coming the other way was a tiny two and a half-year-old named Muffin. When they met each other, each stopped and stared at the other. I could not quite believe my eyes as Murshid became a two and a half year old. His stance, his expression, everything about him became infantile. They stood, hovering in total innocence in space, until Murshid made a mock gesture of disgust, and they went their ways.

Surya

LAMA DRAMA

During those weeks I continued to be alternately impressed and repelled by this enigmatic being. Just when I had decided for the first time to accept him as teacher and take Sufi initiation, he became so crabby that I wondered where the inspiration had possibly come from. I went back and forth for days.

Then one night he asked for questions after his talk. I asked him why he decried Ananda Mai Ma, whom I had seen in India and in whose presence I had entered Samadhi as she stared at me. Finally, unable to bear his critical words, I stomped out of the room into the dark woods towards my tipi. I was pulling myself through the thickest part of the scrub oaks, when she appeared. Not before or since has she appeared as she did then, in clear waking vision. Here she was, Ananda Mai, standing on a sea in dazzling white and smiling at me with deepest love and assurance. Sam had more teaching devices at his command than most educators ever heard about.

Surya

43

THE BIRD OF TIME

After Murshid fell down the steps, and while he was in and out of coma, I dreamt that I was standing before a great classical fountain on which were inscribed the words of Omar Khayyam: THE BIRD OF TIME HAS BUT A LITTLE WAY TO FLY, AND LO — THE BIRD IS ON THE WING. On the other side of the fountain was a large, almost celestial choir in white, singing: SRIDI MA JAI MA, JAI JAI SRI MA with intense devotion for the Holy Mother. Before I was swept away by the music, I noticed that the director of the choir, who had his back to me, was a little man with white hair. He did not need to turn around and wink.

I awoke crying. Any doubts I may have had about Murshid Samuel Lewis as a great teacher and Servant of God had been dispelled.

Surya

ESCALATION

On January 6, hardly a week before Murshid's passing, I had the following dream:

I was in a huge fluorescent department store filled with people doing their last minute shopping on Christmas Eve, when I noticed something unusual. On the upward rising escalator knelt a little man with white hair. Although he was on the escalator, he was not moving. He was kneeling, with his back to me. He was planting prayer feathers, like the American Indians. The plumes were rising, one after another, up the escalator

44

towards the heavens. I watched this procedure for a few minutes. Out of curiosity I walked up to him and tapped him on the shoulder.

Innocently I asked, "Are those eagle feathers?"

"WHAT?" came the gruff reply. (When he turned around, I took him to be a Hassidic Master.) "Do you think I'm *crazy?* Putting *eagle feathers* on an *escalator?*"

Then he said, "Come with me." He took me to the Chan (Chinese Zen Buddhist Center) and showed me every room in the place.

When I later told the dream to Rabbi Zalman Schachter, he interpreted its meaning: "Don't lose the essence in the form."

When I went to write the dream down in the Lama Dream Book, I noticed that a close friend of mine had had a dream that same night about the Great Maggid (an Hassidic Master).

Surya

THE CUP IS BROKEN

The strongest experience I had with Murshid Sam was the moment I heard of his passing. I was in the Lama library when Siddiq made the announcement. Immediately I fell to the ground in *padmasana* (the full lotus) and saw and felt a tremendous golden lotus in my heart. From the lotus came a golden liquid light — which connected with the hearts of all of Murshid's disciples and students . . . a bond unspeakably real.

Surya (Bhakta)

MURSHID'S LAST LETTER
Dictated January 2, 1971

Pir-O-Murshid Sufi Barkat Ali
Lyallpur District, West Pakistan

Praise be to Allah!

This has been a glorious exit, and one which will go down in history, a sign of all the beauty, truth and goodness in the universe.

One has been truly saved from the jaws of death and adversity, and may live on indefinitely as God wills. It is the sign of all symbol and goodness, and the establishment of God's message in the western world forever, praise be to Allah.

For I am the first one born in the west to have received the divine message and believe to have representatives in all the purity and goodness of which Allah is capable and which will now be presumed done forever.

Photo:Mansur

THE GARDENER
LIFE & TIMES

"I am not enthusiastic about the large meeting (of 'holy men') in Boulder. I am far more interested in every dance session you have, in every prayer and ceremony in the Truth Room (Meditation/Prayer Room), and in the least of your folk art projects. While I am not offering direct advice, I feel that when you are pulled by the winds of high-sounding emotional endeavors you may be wasting time and energy. Look after the crops, goats, and now the cow. Then God will bless you directly. At least that is how I feel. Love and Blessings . . ."

Last letter to Lama,
June 1970

(my first poem, written in 1919, age 22)

TO ME HATH BEEN BEEN GRANTED A GARDEN,

Tho only for my care,
To nourish the plants and flowers
That may be growing there.

Twas God that granted this garden,
For only the other day
The owner, my neighbor left it,
To use it, as I may.

And dahlias shall grow in the garden,
and roses of beauty rare,
And daisies and tulips and daffodils,
And poppies and lilies fair.

Yes, there shall be many flowers,
   But not alone will they grow,
But beauty and love and hope and truth,
   These also, shall I sow.

And fairies shall play in the garden,
   Sylphs and elves and gnomes,
And birds shall sing there all day long,
   And make their summer homes.

Yes, and bees shall gather the honey,
   And toil there all the day,
Whilst I shall gather the flowers,
   For that is all my pay.

And what shall be done with the flowers?
   Is the question you may ask,
For after all, they'd only be
   A reward for my daily task.

To, God will have grown these flowers,
   And to God shall they be given,
And I but the steward in that back yard,
   For our Father who art in Heaven.

There'll be some for the poor and lowly,
  And some for those sick in bed,
And others for those in hospitals,
  And for the children whose parents
    are dead.

And so shall all the flowers,
  Be a hope for those whose life
Is shut from the beauties given by God,
  Who are lost in this world of strife.

And everywhere in this garden,
  That God hath granted me,
Shall love be planted and grow,
  And I his servant be.

As for the blossoms that come there,
  A message each shall bring,
Beauty and love and joy and hope,
  And every flower shall sing.

                              Samuel L. Lewis

The GARDENER
LIFE AND TIMES

1896   Sam was born on October 18th, at 2:20 A.M. in San Francisco. His father was Vice-President of the Levi-Strauss Company and his mother was Harriet Rothschild, of the international banking family. As a child, Sam recited from the Bible and other scriptures unknown to his family. His family frowned on his spiritual work when they realized it was not Jewish and that he was not interested in business matters. His mother was more sympathetic to his work than his father was. She would tell the story of the Prophet Samuel and then say of her own son, "He is . . . he was . . . born a prophet and he came in the spiritual body first."

1915   He first became interested in Oriental Philosophy and World Religions at the age of 19 when he visited the booth of the Theosophical Society at the San Francisco World's Fair.

1916   He began studying non-Euclidian geometry and mathematical philosophy under Professor Cassius Keyser of Columbia, who later introduced him to Dr. Alfred Korzybski and thus to general semantics.

1919   At 23 years of age, he returned to California to work with a group of Sufis in Fairfax.

These people had come together to study and practice the teachings of Hazrat Inayat Khan, work which Samuel never abandoned. The group tended to rely on Sam's inner vision even though he was still in his twenties.

1920 He began studying with Sogaku Shaku, a disciple of the Rinzai Zen Buddhist Abbot Shaku Soyen. When Sogaku Shaku was assigned to Hawaii his teaching work was continued by Nyogen Senzaki.

1923 At the age of 27, Sam was initiated into the Sufi Order by Pir-O-Murshid Inayat Khan, the first person to "touch his heart."

1925 During spiritual retreat in Fairfax, Sam received inner initiation from Kwadja Khidr (Elijah) and then all the prophets in turn, culminating with Mohammed.

1926 Six interviews with Hazrat Inayat Khan in Hollywood. He was appointed "Protector of the Message" by this Sufi leader who died the following year.

1926 Nyogen Senzaki, aided by Sam, opened the first official Zendo in the United States (in San Francisco). Sam introduced Paul Reps to Senzaki, *Zen Flesh Zen Bones* resulted.

1927- Served as chief assistant (Khalif) of Murshida
1942 Rabia Martin; gardener and sometime director of Sufi Khankah, Kaaba Allah, in Fairfax, California.

1930 Traveled to New York and received Dharma transmission from Sokei-An Sasaki. Vision of the world's future is first opened.

1937 Studied the yoga of Ramana Maharshi with Paul Brunton.

1944 Rabia Martin died after turning land and organization over to Meher Baba. Sam accepted Baba and endeavored to work within his organization, but withdrew in 1946.

1945 Sam was awarded for service by Army Intelligence (G2) during World War II. He probably worked as an historian and researcher but these activities are clouded in mystery.

1946 In the inner world, Hazrat Inayat Khan turned him over to Prophet Mohammed and Jesus Christ for guidance. He began world peace and food concentrations. Worked in Golden Gate Park, landscaping and collecting refuse. A fire destroyed nearly all of his writings except for *The Book of Cosmic Prophecy*.

1956 Carried out seed-exchange program during his first voyage abroad. In Japan Sam entered samadhi in presence of Roshi Sogen Asahina. He was appointed Fudo, "Protector of the Dharma on Mt. Takao", and was initiated into various Sufi Orders (including Nakshibandhi and Chisti) in Pakistan and India.

1956 Swami (Papa) Ramdas came to San Francisco from South India. He was known as the man who put the Om in OM SRI RAM JAI RAM

JAI JAI RAM. While Papa Ramdas was speaking, Sam played with the children in the lobby. He received personal initiation from Papa Ramdas in India. The Ram mantra inspired many of Murshid's dances in following years.

1960   During his second voyage abroad, he was initiated into the Rifai and Shadhili Orders in Egypt. Sam was accepted as a full Murshid by Pir Barkat Ali of the combined Chisti-Kadri-Sabri Orders in West Pakistan, and was appointed representative of Islamabad University by Pir Dewal Shereef.

1961   Met with India's President Radhakrishnan. Studied with Swami Ranganathananda of Ramakrishna Order; visited with Swami Ramdas.

1962   Returned to America. At this point in his life, he considered his work to be like Moineddin Chisti, who brought Sufism to India.

1966   Initiated his first disciples. Assisted in founding The Holy Order of Man, a mystical Christian school, in San Francisco.

1967   The Voice had manifested and said to Sam: "I make you spiritual leader of the hippies." Ordained "Zen-shi" by Master Kyung-Bo Seo of Korea.

1968   Met Pir Vilayat Inayat Khan, son and successor to his first spiritual teacher. It was Pir Vilayat who encouraged Sam to write down the dances and walks. The meeting of these two men was of great importance for the ailing and divided Sufi Order, which gained new strength and, one might say, a rebirth.

1969 Visited New Mexico and stayed at Lama Foundation for a week; also saw several other communities between Questa and Santa Fe. It seems that this visit marked a major turning point in Murshid Sam's life and work. After many years of rejection by the academic community, he was paid to travel in the fully-accepted role of teacher and guru. He taught the communes and family groups how to dance together, and when he returned to Lama a year later, the dancing had spread through the Taos Valley north into Colorado and south to Albuquerque.

At Lama Foundation Sam found a place where his own teachings were being practiced. Lama's premise, that spirituality is made real by practicality, was Murshid's own message, and the universalist, eclectic approach to spiritual understanding and practice also appealed to him.

Back in San Francisco Sam's work was in full bloom. More and more dances "came" to him, and he had initiated approximately a hundred disciples. "I am now becoming a veritable Pied Piper," he said, "and the more the older and 'respectable' people spurn, the more the young are turning to me, keeping me constantly busy."

1970 On December 28th, shortly before sunrise,

Murshid Sam slipped on the steps in his home and fell, suffering a severe concussion. He was taken to the hospital in a state of shock. For two and a half weeks he was in and out of coma, sometimes unconscious, sometimes delirious and incoherent, and sometimes perfectly clear and rational.

1971 On January 15th, at the age of 75, Sam died in San Francisco. He was buried at Lama Foundation, near Taos, New Mexico.

THE FUNERAL

Beloved of Allah Sufi Barkat Ali,

Honor, love and greetings to you from one of Sufi Ahmed Murad Chisti's disciples, fortunate to be living at the site of his Maqbara. Caliph Moineddin has requested that I describe the funeral service to you.

First to tell you a little of Lama and why our Murshid wished to be buried here. We are a community/school dedicated to the awakening of consciousness, one of a few such places beginning to take root in America, and possibly the only one which welcomes teachers of many different faiths and disciplines. Some of us, after a year's trial, stay here to live; others come for short periods. Murshid came here several times, once with a number of disciples from San Francisco; he lived with us, taught us dancing, walks, prayers, and much about how to live more clearly, joyfully, truly. He felt this place to be a sign of the future, of the "new age" for which he also was an instrument. He also sensed the power of this land and said this is a sacred mountain. Now certainly it is more so, with the presence of his grave here.

The site is about 9000 feet high in a clearing near the path we take up to the higher ridge and peaks. It is surrounded by pine, blue spruce, and cedar trees. Looking out from the spot there is a gap between trees and one can see perhaps a hundred miles across the plain, the gorge of the Rio Grande River, to the mountains of the Continental Divide which mark the "backbone" of this country. Also nearby is the ancient Kiowa Trail used by the Indians to travel north/south.

The night before the funeral ceremony there was inspired singing and chanting in the prayer room here. The coffin rested in the center of the large dome. Different ones visited it in silence. The next morning it was carried up the mountain by six men chanting ALLAH-HO-AKBAR! It was placed on boards over the grave and the funeral service was conducted by Sheikh Daniel Lomax and disciples Mansur and Basira. Mansur walked around everything three times both ways, chanting silently. Then Daniel made the call to prayer which resounded over the mountain loud and pure and joyful! The prayer SAUM was recited, the coffin lowered, and then the prayer SALAT. Then followed a short burial sermon. We all sang the Zikr. Then Basira took a child by the hand, she another, and we formed a long line chanting ALLAH! in and out among the trees. We did a number of the dances Murshid has taught us which were, needless to say, full of feeling. During this time and after, person after person including the children shoveled and threw handfuls of earth into the grave. Also put in were two roses, one from the tomb of Inayat Khan and one from Murshid's home in California. When this was finished the ground was restored as much as possible to its natural state. The grave was marked by stones; at its head was placed a large block of quartz found nearby and the temporary marker carved by disciples in California. The words say:

ON THAT DAY THE SUN WILL RISE IN
THE WEST
AND ALL MEN SEEING WILL BELIEVE.

On top of the grave we placed a bouquet of plants which grow here: sage, juniper, wheat. We knelt in silence for some moments. Several sang a quiet song written for Murshid by his choirmaster. I personally felt a depth of feeling that went from intense personal grief to awe and delight when I saw Murshid dancing on one toe on top of his grave! Laughing! There was (and is) in many of us a sense of intense vibration coming from the spot. During the ceremony the sun had come up the mountain to the spot, and as we walked down the hill we saw a bright crescent moon hanging in the sky.

The Maqbara is watched and cared for. It is visited by disciples, visitors who knew of Murshid, and people here who feel the space.

I hope this report can convey to you some sense of what has happened here for us. It's hard to express how we feel about Murshid — I mean everyone, not just the two of us who are disciples. He took heaviness and turned it into joy! He beat the men at a walking race and fertilized the garden and played with the children. He exhausted us and made us think and argue and dance and bought ice cream. We love him very much! It is a great, great gift to have had his living presence here and now to feel so much the presence of his spirit and the teaching he could give us because he understood so deeply who we are. He broke through our walls when we didn't know he was doing it and many are very surprised! We pray we can continue to unite within ourselves individually and collectively and to shine the light he helped us so much to begin to see.

To you, Pir-O-Murshid, honor, love, and great thanks,

Frances von Briesen (Sahaida)
disciple

FAMILY ALBUM

Jacob Lewis.

Samuel Lewis as a young man.

S.A.M. circa 1930 in Fairfax, California.

ilbert and Sullivan's H.M.S. Pinafore *in San Francisco, 1920's.*

At the tomb of Nizamudin Auliya in Delhi, India, 1956.

In Japan with Buddhist friends, 1956.

Receiving citation from Army Intelligence for work as a historian, W.W. II.

From a Los Angeles paper, 1960: "Samuel L. Lewis (right), Mill Valley horticultural enthusiast and proponent of promoting peace by exchanging trees and seeds . . . presenting a supply of gingko seeds from Japan to the Supervisor of Horticulture for the Los Angeles Recreation and Park Department . . ."

1967.

With Allen Ginsberg.

Dancing in park, San Francisco.

In front of Arboretum, Golden Gate Park, San Francisco, 1968.

On top of Bernal Heights, San Francisco.   *New Years Eve, 1969.*

In front of Mentorgarden,
San Francisco.

In front of Khankah,
Novato, California.

© Photo:Mansur

In the garden.

© Photo:Mansur

With disciples, 1968.

Mens' Ram dance.

Opening of Khankah, Novato, California, October 20, 1968.

Opening of Khankah, Novato, California, October 20, 1968.

Wedding of Michael and Banefsha.

Murshid's funeral, Novato, California: Pir Vilayat conducting Universal Worship.

SAUM

Praise be to Thee, Most Supreme God, Omnipotent, Omnipresent, All-pervading, The Only Being.

Take us in Thy Parental Arms, raise us from the denseness of the earth. Thy Beauty do we worship, to Thee do we give willing surrender, Most Merciful and Compassionate God, the Idealized Lord of the whole humanity. Thee only do we worship, and toward Thee alone do we aspire. Open our hearts toward Thy Beauty, Illuminate our souls with Divine Light. O Thou, the Perfection of Love, Harmony, and Beauty!

All-powerful Creator, Sustainer, Judge and Forgiver of our shortcomings, Lord God of the East and of the West, of the worlds above and below, and of the seen and unseen beings,

Pour upon us Thy Love and Thy Light, give sustenance to our bodies, hearts and souls. Use us for the purpose that Thy Wisdom chooseth, and guide us on the path of Thine Own Goodness. Draw us closer to Thee every moment of our Life, until in us be reflected Thy Grace, Thy Glory, Thy Wisdom, Thy Joy and Thy Peace.

Amen.

SPIRITUAL
ARCHITECTURE

"By 'Spiritual Architecture' is meant that which is accomplished in accordance with sacred principles."

S.A.M.

In "Introduction to Spiritual Architecture," Murshid Sam shows how the builder describes his own being through his work. Architecture is explained as the four dimensionalization of the other arts and also as an esoteric spiritual discipline. Written late in his life as a Commentary on Inayat Khan's "Architecture" in *Yesterday Today and Tomorrow*, this chapter will introduce a work which Lama Foundation hopes to publish in full in the future.

SPIRITUAL ARCHITECTURE

THE SIGNIFICANCE OF ARCHITECTURE

By Spiritual Architecture is meant that which is accomplished in accordance with sacred principles. One can read in the Christian Bible, that when John was in the city of New Jerusalem, there were words inscribed upon it, "The Lord is there," that is to say, that the spirit of the Lord brought the revelation and also that when man feels the Divine Spirit in and around him he may truly experience that bliss which has been symbolised as life in the holy city, Jerusalem.

It is the spirit of God which makes any undertaking spiritual. That which is personal is not holy, unless the Lord is there. The other type of undertaking which can become sacred is that of a group, of which the Bible has said, "When two or three are gathered in My name, there am I in their midst." Such a group undertaking is very important in the spiritual life and blossoms forth in architecture.

Every symbol given to the students of mysticism contains a key to a great cosmic principle. In the esoteric training one learns the meaning of the symbol and its effectiveness in life, both in the manifest and unmanifest aspects. The symbols may be called the 'Alphabet of the Universe.' Masonry is an art and science based on this alphabet; the two aspects of Masonry, speculative and practical or applied, are both based upon it.

The difference between art and architecture is dual, or dualfold. Excepting in the plastic art, work is done in two dimensions and forms are derived out of space instead of being depicted in space. In architecture, outside of planning and blue-printing, the execution is spatial, although the geometry of it is not always the Euclidian, three-dimensional variety. Art, too, is chiefly the work of an individual; architecture, including landscaping and decoration, is the work of a group operating as a unity. This last point is most important and among other things, it points the way toward human brotherhood.

The psychological importance of line and curve and the psychic value of form and shape have not been given much consideration, although from Plutarch to Spengler there have been philosophers who recognize the social significance of the arts and their effects upon mankind. Point, line, circle, square, triangle, cycloid, sphere, cube, pyramid and many other forms have meanings to the mystic, so that one could almost say that there is an esoteric geometry, the study of which may be called geometric symbology. The difference between it and mathematics is important for it can be spelled in life. Dynamic symmetry has been derived from mathematics and applied to art and biology; the same would be true in even a larger sense of geometric symbology.

The great temple of Solomon has stood through the centuries as the ideal pattern for all great temples and sacred architecture. Even today Solomon is revered in many lands and there are multitudes who hope to see someday either the restoration of the temple or the erection of an edifice where all may come to worship and be healed. According to the esoteric traditions the temple of Solomon itself was based upon another temple in the unseen. This temple is described, in a sense, in the book of the Prophet Ezekiel. Many psalms were written in a sense that one may wonder whether they refer to the temple on earth or that in the unseen. It has been supposed that this temple often elevated the consciousness so that one could become aware of that unseen temple.

The method by which Solomon directed the operations in the building of the temple has been a source of wonder. Tradition states that his methods were not different from those used in ancient Egypt and indeed the Egyptians in his day cooperated with him. Much of the work was accomplished in silence. Solomon stood at the head of a great hierarchy. He transmitted his commission (and, it is said, silently) to the Grand Masters, they to the Masters of the various guilds and crafts, who in turn instructed the artists, workers and all hands. It was an application of cosmic and hierarchical law, a supreme brotherhood going to work to accomplish something useful and beautiful. Therefore it has been the source of countless inspirations through the ages.

To recapitulate, one may employ these definitions:

ART is the work of the creative spirit through the individual on two planes;

SCULPTURE is the work of the creative spirit, usually through the individual, on three planes;

ARCHITECTURE is the work of the creative spirit through the collectivity on three planes, or in space;

SPIRITUAL ARCHITECTURE is that which is applied to buildings used for sacred purposes (in all senses);

ESOTERIC OR OCCULT ARCHITECTURE is that based upon a knowledge of symbolism, occultism and esotericism.

For our general purposes one may say that sacred architecture may take on three vital aspects: the group activity which is applied to the building of temples and other grand sacred edifices; the group activity which will be engaged in the construction of khankahs, or inhabitable places; the activity, individual in intent for the building of private homes and small places such as shrines, etc.

Of course there have been many magnificent homes built which impel admiration as marvels of beauty. They need not, however, be regarded as models, both from the standpoint of costs and because they are primarily the source of satisfaction to the few. They are regarded by spiritual students as belonging to *Nufsaniat,* the realm of the satisfaction of individuals. The architecture of the future may bring satisfaction not only to those who dwell in or make use of buildings, but to society as a whole.

The khankah, which is the type of building used by the Sufis of the Orient, offers on its philosophical side, the idea which can be used generally by cooperative groups. It is an alternative to family-home, apartment, hotel and barracks. The khankah in a certain sense becomes a living entity; the persons who dwell there may come and go. So although on the one hand khankahs may be established first for and by spiritual students, there is no reason why the principles of them may not be adopted, for no spiritual teachings are directly against human freedom or the individual's search for happiness.

In the khankah, even in the planning of a khankah, many join in an enterprise. They may complete the architecture and others may adorn the actual building; there can be no individual undertaking in this. Thus between the selection of the ground and the final moving of people into rooms, where there is *as if* one individual working, different people may come and go at different stages, each performing his task or making his contribution. Thus the khankah is dynamic: it lives and grows.

Spirituality also tends toward a greater and ever greater degree of aesthetic expression and human freedom. If there are any restrictions upon the spirit of men, that reveals the predominance of the ego and the extension of *Nufsaniat*. Masonry, in proclaiming God as the Grand Architect of the Universe, has set into motion the opposite spirit, that man, made in the divine image, might reveal the holy spirit in him as he plans and works.

THE MEANING OF ESOTERIC INSTRUCTION

By esoteric instruction is meant not only some secret instruction which is given to the pupil by the teacher, but more especially that which every individual receives by himself in the silence. There is a mistaken view that a spiritual teacher offers some fixed philosophies or ideas to a pupil which the pupil must accept. That has nothing to do with true spirituality, which leads to a type of liberty not experienced by the average man. For when the heart is free, the mind becomes as a tool or willing servant. One may use that tool to affect that which he desires or needs.

The most important practice for the understanding of spiritual architecture is concentration. In the beginning this concentration will not be of different nature from that required from other students, especially students of art. The purpose is to unfold the qualities secluded in the heart, the awakening of which will bring inspiration and a zest for life and work. Then, it is necessary to learn to concentrate with others who are connected with the same enterprise, for, as the Bible teaches, "Whenever two or three are gathered in My name, there am I in their midst."

What is Masonry? It may be regarded as a science and art, which leads to perfection. The ancients saw in nature or *prakriti,* the vast Universe which God gave to man to be moulded into beautiful and useful things. They also saw in *purusha* or spirit, the background of the human spirit which was also to be moulded through character building. The utilization of the atomic materials of the world and the purification of the vibrations of spirit into nobleness and toward perfection was required as one art, one science. And in modern Masonry, especially as explained by Albert Pike, there is a definite effort to unite these two aspects. And concerning these Jesus Christ has said: "Be ye perfect, even as your Father in Heaven is perfect."

Therefore spiritual architecture includes not only the planning and construction of buildings, but a series of processes, applied in one's private life in order to do this work perfectly, which results incidentally in character-building and human perfection. One does not always emphasize the faults of human nature or the frailties of individuals. One finds through concentration and other esoteric exercises which lead one constantly toward the ideal, the framework for the betterment of nature and human nature together.

In India the *Silpa Shastra* was written as the

basic law for the craftsmen engaged in sacred undertakings. It was considered that no man has the right to build a temple or even an altar or to take part in these works unless he himself had a certain training, indeed belonged to a certain caste. The caste rules even from birth were of such a nature that he was supposed to have come to a realization of the divine spirit in himself and behave accordingly.

Today we need not follow the *Silpa Shastra*, although a study of it may throw some light upon the methods used in ancient times, which can always be elaborated upon. But we now have so many materials that can be used in construction: endless varieties of wood and metals, glass, adobe, bricks and masonry materials, and constantly the results of the technology of the day. Although living materials (e.g. woods) have more life and more magnetism, where beauty is concerned one should not be too restricted. The whole earth is there for man to use.

Again today direct handicraft is not so much in evidence. There was a time when the handworker was needed. Today the machine has taken his place. Yet the creative spirit can never be expressed satisfactorily through a machine. The artist will always be needed; there are things hands can do, especially under inspiration, that nothing else can do. Besides, a spiritual revival may help to revive old handcrafts and to introduce art-forms from one nation to another; e.g. flower and plant arrangement, landscape gardening, interior decorating, etc.

Today the knowledge of the world has been spread from country to country and advantage is being taken of it so that there is a departure from tradition and uniformity. Although in a certain sense this has been productive of anarchy, it also gives such scope for planning and methods, that perhaps never before were there so many opportunities in this field, cost alone preventing wide-spread experimentation.

Therefore one may see the cube, pyramid, cross, circle, sphere, star and all the elements of symbolism and geometry employed in building. Adaptations have been made from Egyptian, Greek, Roman, Siamese, Burmese, Chinese, Hindu and other architectures. The distant past, the less remote past and the preceding periods alike offer ideas which can be used, employing perhaps other materials for building as science offers them to man. Thus, so far as form and material are concerned, there seems no end to freedom excepting the laws of nature and engineering.

What is needed, therefore, is an equal freedom of the spirit to counterbalance and dominate this material freedom. Only the people of the day have lost their ability to meditate and relax. And it is of little value to copy ancient external methods without also using their styles of self-discipline and preparation. Even now Japanese craftsmen practice meditation and concentration.

When we look at the architecture of the past we recognize at once that the most beautiful examples are connected with religion. In those days castles were built for military purposes, not for beauty, and even in times of peace the masses were otherwise excluded from opportunities for self-expression in aestheticism. Koran and Bible and *Saddharma-unkarika Sutra* offer suggestions, which have inspired devotees. Cathedral and temple and mosque and pagoda have been built. Those who undertook such works were inspired by the ideals of love, harmony and beauty, each in his own way. No wonder one learns: "Zen (spiritual meditation) *is* everyday life."

The Sufis have especially devoted themselves to this field. The shrines of Islam have often been built by them, and the care of these shrines has been in their hands. Where religions have touched, as Christianity and Islam in Turkey, the Sufis protected the holy places of both. In India there are holy places of the Hindus which are guarded by Sufis.

There is a story of a young boy who wished *bayat* (investiture into Sufism, also called initiation). He was told by the Murshid (director) that he was not ready and he should work for a certain smith for a year. He went to work and at the end of the year was summoned by the teacher. "What have you learned?" "Oh, I know how to handle the bellows and look after the fire and shape metals." "Is that all? Well, go back and come here at the end of next year." This the lad did and returned at the end of another year at the teacher's request.

"What did you learn this last year?" The boy answered, "I know how to shoe a horse and to make armor and do all that is required of the smith." "I am so sorry," said the teacher, "but there is still more to learn." The boy did not understand, but obeyed. He worked one year more and then he rushed to the teacher and said, "Thank you dear Murshid, for the marvelous instructions."

It seems that all the time he had been living close to the smith, breathing the same atmosphere, adopting the same rhythm, doing things in the same way. The smith was a master but like all true masters was hidden (ghaib). He was following the path known by Sufis as *rind*. The very attunement between instructor and apprentice awakened the heart of the latter and thus he learned that which cannot be found in books. He had discovered the "way."

The House of Tansen

Let my soul become
a flute, beloved,
my body a flute
of reed,
Let my being
be aroused in song
and the song become my deed,
Let the glory of God assert itself,
now that I've come so far,
Let the music of life come through
my mouth,
just like a morning star,
Let the star prepare the world itself
for the coming of the sun,
Let the flute assert, assert itself,
the music has begun.
The empty self, O empty one,
may the prayer become the deed,
The soul has become a flute my lord,
my body a flute of reed.

S.A.M.

Tansen was the renowned court musician of the Indian
Emperor Akbar, a Sufi.

THE BOOK of

HEART

Do not proclaim the
  conceivable,
The God of many attributes and
  powers;
Nor do I proclaim the
  inconceivable,
Vainly sought by the wandering
  mind,
Supershadowed by words.
But I proclaim the
  superconceivable—
Who is to be loved.

Which is nearer to infinity,
The long time or the short time?
The long time is not nearer to infinity,
Neither is the short time nearer to infinity—
Love is closest to infinity.

What is this human heart, beyond mind, beyond
　　logic, beyond explanation?
What is this human heart, irresponsive
　　to infinitude,
Completely unaffected by finitude,
By means of which distant lovers may commune,
By means of which proximate enemies are
　　brought to confusion,
By means of which understanding is
　　immediately expanded,
Where space and time and the might of man
　　are of no avail,
Where the smile of a little infant may
　　be all-conquering?

What is the distance between the stars of space?
What is the distance between the dreams of lovers?
What is the distance between the points of heart?

What is nameable, what is intelligible,
　　what is logical—
What has it brought thru the course
　　of many centuries?
What is describable, what is commendable,
　　what is proclaimed,
What has it done through the period
　　of many centuries?
Where is the seat of compassion
　　within the consciousness?
Where is the source of mercy
　　within the consciousness?
What have these to do with what has gone before?

When the world has been seized
  in uttermost turmoil,
When the greatest hopes of diplomats
  end in frustration,
When the dreams of lofty minds only
  reach an impasse,
When the most carefully worked out plans only
  end in naught,
Who looks into the ever beating heart?
Who seeks the kingdom which lies
  so dormant within?
Who has discovered the luminous Pearl
  beyond all prices?

What Alexis Carrel did with the heart of flesh,
What Gautama Buddha did with the heart of mind,
What Jesus Christ did with the heart of heart—
Shadows come and go, enter and depart,
Substance remains eternally.

When heart pulses to the radiations of the
  universe,
When atoms dance and waves sparkle in unison,
When the sense of Godness becomes a reality
  where we stand,
When the feeling of compassion is all-embracing,
Where need we look for an answer to our dilemma?

92

Come, young people and I shall sing of true love,
Come, young people, and heed the notes of my song,
For when you love one another to the exclusion
   of everything else,
When you love one another and are blind
   to the rest of the world,
That is passion, that is infatuation, that is
   the quickening of the ego.
When you love one another to the inclusion
   of everything else,
When you love one another and your eyes see
   the rest of the world,
When you love one another and grow abundantly
   in that love,
That is the divine presence in your midst,
This leads to the marriage hallowed by eternity.

On the battlefield of Kurukshetra,
In the long ago, in the not so long ago, in
   the ever present,
The Lord of Heart assumed supreme command

Nearer to us than breathing, closer than
   hand and feet,
Even more proximate than the jugular vein—
Forced from our consciousness by those
   who attain position,
Driven from our minds by those who
   have secured power,
Smothered by the authorities, who would

exercise their sway,
Yet untrammeled, undiminished, not even modified
By those ignorant multitudes who have stood
    before the world as mediators,
For nothing stands between God
    and the human heart,
Nothing tarnishes the altar within the heart.

O for a single bath in that supreme fountain of light,
For a single ray of that unfathomable love,
For even a momentary touch of the
    Supreme Awfulness,
Attaining peace, neither life nor death
    would matter
Attaining bliss, one attains the all.

Photo:Mansur

SPIRITUAL PRACTICES

SPIRITUAL PRACTICES

includes the following five sections:

1. PAPERS ON THE WALK
2. DIVINE ATTRIBUTE WALKS
3. THE DANCE
4. BREATH
5. MEDITATION

"Sufic and other spiritual practices do not bring Grace. For in truth, Grace is always there. Every human soul is always under Divine Grace but does not know it; therefore the practices."

S.A.M. "Sangathas on Breath"

Sam met people on their levels. Some of his followers had the feeling that they were teaching *him*. He could easily say, with Inayat Khan, "I learn more from my mureeds (disciples) than they learn from me." Religion and philosophy were important to Sam only in how they helped guide people to God. Thus could the teachings illuminate the day-to-day life of the mureeds. The Way of the Sufi is not to worship the guru but to unite with him through attunement. Attracted by the energy of the Dance, the early disciples soon discovered that there was much more to Sufism than joyful dancing. Through Walks and Breath concentrations, Murshid Sam taught tassawuri (emulation). There are stages in Sufism: first the student emulates his own teacher; then he attunes to the Prophets, each in turn, ending with Mohammed — the Complete Man. Then, like Mohammed, he effaces into Allah, beyond form, and is reborn as a servant of God in this world. The process of *fana* (dissolution) and *baka* (resurrection) corresponds to the path of the Bodhisattva which goes through emptiness and returns, through knowledge and compassion, to "chopping wood and carrying water," which life in this world requires.

This section is a compilation of spiritual practices which Murshid gave from 1967 to 1971, including instructions in Sufi dancing, an esoteric manual on Breathing, and two poetic descriptions of meditation.

WALK

There are walks under karma and there are the walks under salvation. These two stand distinct. The walks under karma can be analyzed and learned and mastered, or they can master us. The walks under salvation can be learned and mastered but not analyzed. When you were in love could you analyze the walks you took to your beloved? Can you analyze the walks your child first took with you?

S.A.M.

TOWARD THE ONE, THE PERFECTION OF
LOVE, HARMONY, AND BEAUTY, THE
ONLY BEING, UNITED WITH ALL THE
ILLUMINATED SOULS, WHO FORM THE
EMBODIMENT OF THE MASTER, THE
SPIRIT OF GUIDANCE.

papers on the walk

WALK

Walking is one of the first arts which can be taught to children. It is not usually looked upon as an art, but in the teaching of children how to draw and also how to dance, some knowledge of Walking as an art or even as a science is helpful. We do not usually take this seriously, and we do not see that without some knowledge there is not only uncontrolled fatigue but also emotional problems arise.

The principle of Path appears in several religions. It is not only in their mystical aspects but in many ceremonies and rituals. Circumambulation of an altar or shrine is also important, even regarded as an important act of devotion. The very word 'path' signifies that which comes from the feet treading — it almost means 'what is footed.' It is now important to study the Walk both as a physical exercise and as a super-physical endeavor, making both movement and rest the most fundamental things in life.

No doubt out of walking came circumambulation and other rituals and these all culminated in pilgrimages of some sort. And in many rituals or pilgrimages the shoes are discarded — even sometimes one is compelled to go barefoot. Although Moses was told to take off his shoes because he was on holy ground, both the ritual and its importance have been lost in the West.

In Sufism it is stressed that the physical body is the temple of God. This was also taught by Jesus Christ in both the scriptures and in other writings attributed to him. The substitute of an institution as an important structure, and the by-passing of Man as the creature of God, and the non-acceptance of his being created in the divine image has set all religion off in the wrong direction.

One thing almost obvious in the consideration of Walk is that the feet themselves are connected with shrines. When one does the "lotus" and other postures the human body is the shrine and the feet an external shrine; then there is Walking. But if one agrees with Kabir that God is everywhere, one can learn in Walk that the body is the real temple and that every place is a holy shrine.

With this attitude we not only learn to walk but also to overcome fatigue without giving any consideration to the fatigue. The Hebrew Bible states that the Creator does not slumber nor sleep and not only whoever is conscious of the Divine Presence, but even every organ of the body, filled with divinity, will be able to function as if belonging to Eternity rather than to time.

It should be recognized that before we can run we must be able to walk, and by the same token even before we walk we should be able to breathe. If one ambles, if one slouches, one does not manifest magnetism. From the very beginning of discipleship talibs (intermediate disciples) in Sufism are given the instructions in breathing which aid in increasing both magnetism and the capacity for vitality.

One can understand some of this with music and its effect; especially the effects of marches, whether military or not. They impel the body to walk . . . to walk in rhythm (a second item) and to feel vitality (a third item). This gives some idea as to how to increase magnetism. And the first thing which should be learned is to *breathe in rhythm*.

We can learn from the infants who use rattles and drums and metal objects which supply rhythm. Melody is something else and is concerned with mind, but at an early age before the mind is properly developed the children respond to rhythm and make rhythms themselves.

The use of rhythms helps one to walk and to walk properly. The other thing needed is posture. We require it in repose, in the practices of meditation; we require dynamic posture in walking to have the back straight and the back perpendicular. Someone [Paul Reps] has written on 'back breathing' and this is proper when the currents go from the base of the spine upward. It has untold advantages and yet is one of the most fundamental and simple things in life.

Therefore one of the first lessons is the proper

posture, the proper breathing, the proper rhythm. And these help also to overcome fatigue.

It is more necessary to *feel* than to think about one's movements. Thinking about action alone can become a wearing thought and use up the mental magnetism. But if the mind is permitted to wander too much one can lose direction. Therefore in the practice known as Walking Fikar one must have a particular path, preferably a straight line, and it should be in fields or what are called 'jungles' in the Orient, meaning where one does not meet people or vehicles.

If one has a goal, physical or mental, while walking, it brings all the magnetism together. It is a living concentration. For instance a loving person going to meet his or her beloved is endowed and imbued with a living spirit which makes action easier, and fatigue disappears. If we practice a "Toward the One," whatever be the goal or purpose, walking becomes much easier. And therefore also sacred phrases may be thought or repeated, consciously or unconsciously.

SPIRITUAL WALK

The spiritual walk is one connected with esoteric training and development. It may be begun in the Buddhist fashion by simply counting breaths, a fixed number, or a certain number. Or it may be done in the Sufi fashion which is not too different, excepting there are accepted cycles like 4, 10, 14, 21, 33, 100 or 101, etc.

102

Very often it is a good idea to encourage applicants and neophytes to walk and to watch the breath. This is the actual discipline in some Orders. What is most important is to learn the relationship between God and man, between breath and life, and thus pass beyond the gates of so-called "death."

Then one should breathe concentrating on "Toward the One" with both inhalation and exhalation, the same phrase. This can be done best by leaning on the breath, but also one can take so many steps to each breath. This is somewhat more complicated. In between comes listening to music, wherein the rhythm is most important. Besides those who have had training in meditation and this Darood (Toward the One, etc.) will find it easier and more comfortable. It comes naturally.

Zen Buddhism says that Zen is everday life. It is not so when we make a doctrine of it. It is so when we practice it at all times. People everywhere find walking a part of their everyday life.

It is several years since Sam said to Ruth St. Denis, "Mother, I am going to revolutionize the world."

"What are you going to do?"

"I am going to teach the little children how to walk."

She jumped up: "You have it! You have it!"

Diaries, July 3, 1968

USE OF CENTERS

Hara is a Japanese word for centering in the solar plexus and bundle of nerves in the abdominal region. It is used much by those who practice meditation. Meditation has been taught sitting in lotus posture and this often tires or fixates certain muscles. The muscles have to be unstrung. There must not be this tension too long.

There are lazy people both in the Orient and Occident who devote much time to sitting. Some even are under the delusion that sitting is spiritual emancipation and has a connection with samadhi.

Sufis sometimes use the symbol of Dot and Circle which is emblematic of contraction and expansion. The *Hara* walk is essentially a contractive walk and it brings all the benefits of this contraction. It helps in concentration; it helps to synthesize and to produce what has been called "integration of personality." Those who practice *Hara* are certainly of one piece.

They do not have wandering minds. As they keep the body under control, at the same time they are keeping the mind under control and this builds up the will. It also makes possible long endeavor and so is another mode of overcoming fatigue.

This Hara corresponds to the negative side of LA ILLAHA EL IL ALLAH*(there is nothing but God). This is called fana by Sufis and helps toward self-effacement. It has been assumed, and wrongly

* this was how S.A.M. recited the zikr. The traditional form is LA ILLAHA ILL' 'LLAH.

assumed, that this negative effacement also produces liberation. That is only one side of it. Besides no mechanical means, no rules, no rituals, nothing controlled by man alone can liberate man. But at the same time it brings the control of *nafs*, the ego, and its benefits are enormous.

The Sufis and some advanced Zen Buddhists use the Heart center. They use it in walking and meditation. It is always beneficial to practice a silence before effort, walking or gymnastics or dancing or anything, and feel the breath, learn the ways of breathing and then practice the centering.

Some of these practices are found in *Zen Flesh, Zen Bones*. Many of them emphasize the Heart-centering. Nevertheless it is advantageous to practice the muscular Hara, to integrate the body as well as the personality and this can be done by walking either in the presence of a teacher or by examples set forth by a teacher.

If we study the lives of dancers, especially in this modern age since centering has been discovered in the West, we can see advantages and disadvantages. Isadora Duncan discovered the solar plexus center and used it. She did not have any teacher; she just used it and unwisely abused herself. She became more emotional and uncertain. Her life reflected her dancing and her dancing her life.

At the opposite end was the great Nijinski, who used the head center. He could almost levitate. He rose from the denseness of the earth. His body became ethereal, and at the same time his mind became ethereal. Like Isadora Duncan he was unbalanced but in the opposite direction.

It is unwise to practice with the centers in the head for the purpose of walk until one has practiced with at least the *Hara* center. This gives balance. Sufism constantly emphasizes balance but the mentally-minded people think if they have these words and these thoughts they have something. They have nothing until they are able to control centers and not be controlled by them. Knowledge of breath is important; it may even be more important than centering (see *On Breath*).

Centering has a glamour which breathing does not, yet breathing is fundamental to life; we cannot live without it. So the pupil should certainly practice *Hara* and then when the hold of *Hara* is very great, under wise guidance head-centering may be tried. But if not, then Heart-centering. For after all, the Heart center is near the center of the body, and also in the unseen it is near the center of personality.

Besides there are certain attributes and qualities which manifest physically through different organs. If this were not so the animal world would not have advanced, for in the lower creatures all functions are found in miniscule in all the cells. Differentiation and evolution and advancement all go together.

This would suggest that there is centering in abdomen, a centering in head and a centering in thorax near heart, and each has its purpose. But as people are weak mostly they have to begin with *Hara*. After they are strong they can practice with heart-centering and there is no end to advantage.

Head centering is mostly needed to increase Joy, Bliss, Lightness, rising above the denseness of earth and material-mindedness. But one should not become the slave of it; one is not necessarily more "spiritual" because one becomes more ethereal.

THE FEET

When we become concerned with centers, we are likely to suppose that some parts of the body are more to be venerated than others. There is a lesson in the First Epistle to the Corinthians in the Christian Bible to the contrary. The body is the temple of the divine Spirit. It has become part of the Sufi Message to emphasize this.

No doubt it is easier to impress people with abdomen-centering and heart-centering and head-centering. But Sufis have always been taught to watch their feet, and that they are treading on God's earth.

There are breathing and other practices by which one learns to feel the magnetism go out the feet. This can be tried sitting at first, and perhaps best with only the rear of the feet on the ground (the heel). Then one can feel the magnetism while standing and afterwards while walking. One can concentrate on the feet.

The Japanese, concentrating on the abdomen, rid their minds of useless luggage. The ridding of luggage is more important than the method. *What is needed is a method that works, not a philosophy about a method, which can be very confusing.*

As one feels the breath go out the feet, this also helps one to overcome fatigue and to feel courage and direction. This also impels the breath to be felt through the whole body. Then the body acts as one. One has a whole body and the whole body is the Divine Temple.

It has been taught that the last shall be first. We may begin with the head; we end with the feet. Each can produce the sense of oneness and this sense of oneness is most important in every school of spiritual development.

"His training enabled many of us to become proficient walkers. We used to go to Saturday afternoon walk classes in San Francisco. We would walk to places when the class was small. We walked to Ching Wa Lee's art studio in China Town. We walked to the Japanese garden in Golden Gate Park. We walked to the Arboretum. We walked to the Fine Arts Museum. We walked to the Rose Garden and we walked to Shakespeare Garden, all in Golden Gate Park. But when the classes got larger we walked around the block and danced in the park across the street."

(Mansur)

PREVENTION OF FATIGUE

The attributes of God (Allah) may be used to help overcome any shortcoming. Loss of breath is actually one of the greatest shortcomings. We do not notice it. We find many people who are very emotional, who are selfish, who are inconsiderate, who do not breathe correctly. When we get them to take slow rhythmical inhalations and exhalations, it has a profound effect on character changes. This is because, as the Bible teaches but unfortunately religion does not accept, "God is Breath."

The phrase YA HAYY! may be translated 'O Life!' But it is not 'O Life!' as a mere thought. The very vowel effects show that the life is connected with both breath and vowel formation. People who are subject to fatigue easily, who cannot carry out any project because the mind wanders, benefit by repeating audibly or mentally this phrase YA HAYY!

In practice there are two ways to use it. One is on the inhalation, every time one starts to breathe in to think this phrase; the other is to think it every time one takes a step with the right foot. Either method has some advantage.

A slightly more complicated exercise is to think YA HAYY YA HAKK, which roughly means 'O Life, O Truth.' Actually the K or gutteral sound helps to bring the effectiveness down to earth. If people repeat YA HAYY often they could be drawn above the denseness of the earth, even to ecstasy. For many this is good, especially in the material civilization. For the young this is also good, for they live in a less dense atmosphere.

But by repeating in sound or thought "YA HAYY YA HAKK" one keeps a balance, not too much inwardness and not too much outwardness. One might almost add that people who are extroverted by nature gain from YA HAYY and people who are introverted by YA HAKK; but for a group it is best to use the phrases together.

In Walk this must be done mostly by thought until one is well aware of their effectiveness, how they control and magnetize the breath. If this basic lesson is learned it will help much more when persons or groups advance to rituals and dances.

"In India initation may consist entirely in receiving a mantram from a spiritual teacher. The devotee accepts the phrase as coming from God, as being God, and practices repeating the mantram continuously. Many, including my own Guru, Papa Ramdas, have come to full God-realization thru this simple method. I am absolutely free to give with my blessing two such phrases to anyone to repeat: OM SRI RAM JAI RAM JAI JAI RAM and ALLAH."

Diaries - June 10, 1968

TASSAWURI

Tassawuri is an advanced practice and requires a teacher, usually a living teacher. One does best by performing Tassawuri either in the presence of a living teacher, or when one has a firm impression of the teacher in mind it can be done in his absence; or when the teacher manifests and brings a great blessing, Tassawuri can be performed easily.

There are several ways of acquiring Tassawuri. One is to see the teacher and even follow the teacher while he walks. Another is to be deeply impressed, so that one is aware of the teacher's rhythm.

There are practices in concentration called MURAKKABA which enable the devotee to advance along this line. Practices mean practices and not thoughts about such subjects. These thoughts are often the gates to the worst kind of delusions and self-centeredness. People have the philosophies and neither knowledge nor wisdom. They do not know if they really can get into the rhythm of the teacher.

Sufic concentration (Murakkaba) requires devotion. Love, devotion and attunement are the best requirements. Then one feels, sometimes even sees the teacher, so to speak, without any physical contact. So one usually starts with the living teacher. One gets into the rhythm of the teacher. But at the same time the teacher may not be perfect, and he in his turn may be practicing the rhythms of Rama or Krishna, or Shiva or Buddha, or Moses or Jesus or Mohammed.

There is another form of Tassawuri in the circumambulation of shrines. This has reached its highest degree in walking about the Kaaba at Mecca with Tassawuri Mohammed (Effacement into the Prophet, may Allah's Blessings be upon Him). This no doubt is the highest, hardest and also most rewarding practice. But being highest and hardest it is like walking up a steep cliff, and it is better to learn to walk first, then climb slopes.

Once one learns the principle, then it can be applied in many ways.

There is another way called AKHLAK ALLAH, which is to feel God, to feel that one is in His Presence, that one is walking within Him and He is walking within one. This is a most beneficial practice, and everybody can learn to do it.

DIVINE ATTRIBUTE WALKS

"Now it becomes very important to speak on the Divine Name and from the Sufi standpoint to repeat the SIFAT-I-ALLAH, which are called 'The Beautiful Names of God.' Whenever anybody has a problem we repeat the Name that will help that person."

Diaries – Aug. 28, 1967

The practice of the Sifat-i-Allah (Qualities of Allah) combines feeling, movement, and recitation of sacred phrases. They may be considered meditations in action. While walking, feel the manifestation of each quality in your own being. The phrases are recited in Arabic (though Hebrew may be substituted). It is important to know the English meaning of each name.

The positioning of the hands should be carefully regarded, as it is, insofar as possible, in accord with psychic law. Begin by repeating the Bismillah: "BISMILLAH ER-RAHMAN, ER-RAHIM."

ER-RAHMAN
The Compassionate
Hands in front at waist level, palms down, radiating.

ER-RAHIM
The Merciful
Hands in front at waist level, palms up, receiving, empathizing.

YA JAMIL
O Beauty;
God is Beautiful
and loves Beauty.
Palms down, hands gently move outward and downward, gracefully, massaging the air.

YA MALIK
O King of Kings
Determined and majestic walk, arms swing freely, voice strong.

YA AZIM
O Highest

> Arms lifted above head, straight up as far as possible, but open, Allah is beyond the mind.

YA QUDDUS
O Holy One

> Palms together as in prayer, holiness all around.

YA FATTAH
O Opener of the Way

> Emphasis on the Ah sound. Hands to breast, then sweeping open and out, a rapid motion; feel door opening.

YA GHAFOOR
O Forgiver

> Hands move out from heart, as if blessing everyone.

114

YA WADOOD
O Loving

Hands clasped over heart, then opening up into a cup, offering love. Sound the final D.

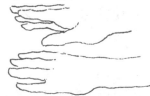

YA HAYYOO
YA QAYYOOM
O Ever-Living,
O Eternal!

Hands held high, palms together, coming down to heart and spreading out, then back to top.

YA SHAFEE
YA KAFEE
O Healer,
O Remedy

Arms outstretched toward center of circle. slightly down, extending magnetic blessing of health to a person sick standing in center (3 times). Do after other attributes.

SUBHAN ALLAH
God is Pure;
Glory be to God
>Hands clasped in front, below waist; humility, devotion, head bowed.

AL-HAMDU LILLAH
Praise be to God
>Arms lifted upward with opening motion above head; heart energy rises.

ALLAHO AKBAR
There is no power or might save in God
(Peace is Power)
>Turn facing inward in circle; right arm under the left of person to right; move counterclockwise; strong voice, peaceful.

Variations on these concentrations and on the other attributes include their expansion into music and free dance.

© Photo:Mansur

© Photo:Mansur

Photo: William B. Giles

"PIR MAULANA SAYS:

This Breath is the
One that Counts."

S.A.M.

THE DANCE

"One of the reasons I am teaching this music and dancing is to increase Joy, not awe towards another person, but bliss in our own self. This is finding God within, through Experience."

"Sam hears that his dances are now spreading like wildfire. He has no monopoly and no copyright. . . . Heart calls to heart and soul to soul."

Diaries — December 14, 1969

It was the Dance which attracted people to Sam. They were drawn by the joy and brotherly feeling surrounding the sessions, and they were also drawn to Sam who by then was as old as most of their grandfathers. Although he was an awesome intellectual with a tremendous range of knowledge, this was not what attracted the young. The meetings were often held in Sam's home or in the park nearby, and he loved to cook for "his children." The lectures and Sufi classes were sometimes followed by ice cream.

HOW TO DANCE

Here are some keys which will help the Dancing be more meaningful for you. To do even one or two of these will have quite a profound effect:

1. LISTEN. Do not simply recite the mantram. Listen to the other people (other yourselves) recite it too. Listen to the person directing the Dance. When you begin to listen, your voice will automatically begin to harmonize. Find the center of the sound.

2. FEEL. The Dances are designed to take us more and more into the universe of feeling. Resist the impulse to think; stay with your own feelings. If you go off into the world of thoughts don't judge yourself, simply bring your concentration back to feeling. If you can do this the Dances will serve to refine and purify your emotional life.

3. CONCENTRATE ON THE SACRED PHRASE. The sacred phrase, sometimes called *Wazifa* or *Mantra*, centers the Dance. We all say this together. The GRACE of Allah can operate through the sacred phrase. . . if we are willing to receive it, to let it be. With each repetition feel the phrase touching your being in a deeper and deeper way.

4. DON'T BE AFRAID TO STOP THE DANCE. This is especially for leaders. If the Dance gets out of control, or just isn't making it, it is much better to stop and begin anew. Learning is more important than just doing.

5. SIMPLE, RHYTHMIC MUSIC. This can be a great aid, guitar and drum especially. Musicians should emphatically resist going off on their own trip. For a musician the mantram must be uppermost in his concentration. The music should accentuate the natural rhythm of the mantram (sacred phrase). Drummers especially must bear this in mind! The simpler the better. Don't dominate the space. The sacred phrase should by far be the loudest sound. If you play your instrument correctly, no one will even notice you. Isn't that wonderful?

6. MOVE TOGETHER. Restrain your exuberance to make an individualistic exhibition. You will be amazed how much higher the Dances are when you use that same energy to harmonize with the others in the circle. Your sense of yourself as a

separate ego-entity will disappear if you can do this. Feel your body fully. Then, gradually, or suddenly, *become the whole circle*.

7. WATCH YOUR BREATH. Breath is life. Breath is movement. Voice is breath. Let breath B R E A T H E.

8. ECSTASY. These Dances can lead to states of ecstasy. Joyously High! How invigorating to feel this way! When you're in the center of the circle, especially, soar. But soar with your whole being. Taste all the planes *at the same time*. This is called stereoscopic vision. You don't have to lose consciousness of the earth plane (your own body). You can feel like a lead instrument in a great improvisational symphony: you can accentuate your own notes but always in harmony with all the other notes. Find the keynote.

9. DEVOTION. This is a *grace*. To willingly submit ourselves to Allah in Whom we live and move and have our being. Hypocrisy may be the only sin. But how wonderful it is when we actually feel like bowing before the eternal truth in humility. These Dances can be worship: the *celebration of the Presence of Allah*. Know that even if you don't see Him, verily He sees you.

10. AMIN (ah-meen). This means "so be it" ('Svaha' in Sanskrit). We say this at the conclusion of many Dances. The important thing is not to *say* it, but to mean it, to affirm with one's whole being.

11. SILENCE. There may be a silent meditation before the Dance starts but if the participants are not veterans in this they may learn the meditation through dancing and also learn the dancing through meditation. After the sound and music of the Dance stop, then *enter the silence*. This is your opportunity to hear what has been created. In this silence one can absorb all the qualities evoked during the Dance. This is the most important part of the Dance. It becomes all-encompassing.

Beloved Ones of Allah, all these words are just in hopes of you falling awake and finding the truth in your own self. Sufism is based on experience and not on premises. You know your own experience better than anyone else. Be true to that. Don't let anyone pull the wool over your eyes; neither be swayed from what you know by the opinions of others.

Editor

THE INTRODUCTORY BISMILLAH DANCE

This is usually the first Dance performed in an assembly. All those present hold hands in a circle and recite the Sufi Invocation. Even persons who may not be able to participate in the Dance for whatever reason should join together for the invocation:

This phrase may be repeated three times if you like. It should be concentrated upon. There is much meaning in it. Then the group recites: "BISMILLAH, ER-RAHMAN, ER-RAHIM." And in English, "We begin in the Name of Allah, Most Merciful and Compassionate."

1. Hands joined and moving counterclockwise, all chant "ALLAH." (two syllables; emphasis on the 2nd syllable), 10 times.
2. Raise arms, *all together*, saying "ER-RAHMAN"; Lower arms, *all together*, saying "ER-RAHIM."
3. Repeat "ALLAH" 4 times with hands joined and down. Then #2 is repeated. All together there are 4 repetitions of this cycle.
4. A new cycle of four is begun and "ALLAH" is chanted 4 times; then the leader calls out "half-turn." All turn together, arms free and up, saying "ER-RAHMAN," joining hands as they come down "ER-RAHIM." Continue

127

walking and chanting the next four "ALLAH"s. This half-turn cycle is also repeated 4 times. (The second time will find everyone facing inward again.)

5. The leader then calls out "Full turn." "Turn and a half." "Two turns," and even "Three complete turns." All these are cycles of four.

6. The last movement is for everyone to spin ("All spin"), saying "ER-RAHMAN, ER-RAHIM," concluding with all saying "AMIN," with hands in prayer position. (The spin is optional and not desirable when there are persons present who are not yet proficient at it.)

RAM NAM DANCES

In each Dance the Sanskrit mantram "OM SRI RAM JAI RAM JAI JAI RAM" is repeated. Where there are changes of movement the mantram is repeated in cycles of 4. Circles move in a counterclockwise direction. Feel the phrase in your heart. Feel Divine Love. Don't press by getting excited and trying hard. Let the breath flow.

RAM NAM DANCE for circles of five.

Each syllable of the Ramnam gets full weight. It is very important to keep all the circles in harmony with each other. This involves *listening* — a most important spiritual practice. Circles are composed of two men and three women or three men and two women. At the end of the four cycles described above the 'twos' change places; thus everyone will touch everyone else in the Dance. The cycles are then repeated. This can go on any number of times. But if the rhythm begins to falter and the circles get out of phase the Dance should be brought to a close, or it should be stopped and begun again.

1. Hold hands around circle, begin moving. (4 repetitions)
2. Swing held hands as circle moves. *(Keep in rhythm. 4 repetitions)*.
3. Alternate hands inside circle, i.e. hold hands with the person beyond the person immediately next to you. Don't cross your hands.
4. Duck under; hands now alternating on outside circle.
5. At the end of the Dance all put arms around persons on either side, and move circle around very rapidly, leaning back, chanting "OM SRI RAM JAI RAM JAI JAI RAM."
6. The Dance should come to a clear conclusion. Much energy has been aroused and should not be dispersed by excited conversation. Instead the circles should stay close together, while all bring their breaths back to a gentle focus, thus *assimilating* what has been created.

RAM NAM DANCE for any number.

1. Hold hands around circle. (4 repetitions)
2. Swing held hands.
3. Egyptian position. Hands held; elbows make 90 degree angle; head moves right to left, left to right.
4. Place hands on shoulder on either side.
5. Cycles may be repeated any number of times. End by saying "OM HARI OM."

BUDDHIST NEM-BUT-SU DANCE

This is best done as a partner dance. All move in a line of counterclockwise direction repeating:NAMO AMIDA BUT-SU (Hail to the Buddha of the Western Paradise).

1. The left hand clapped over the right to the right side saying "NAMO AMIDA." Then the right hand over the left to the left side saying "BUT." Then the left over the right to the right side saying "SU." The rhythm should be such that "NAMO AMIDA" is four beats and "BUT" and "SU" each two beats, approximately. The series is repeated four times.
2. Now the right hand is clapped over the left as above. The above series is thus repeated, but reverses, so one begins on the left side.
3. Women turn around facing the men and walk backwards. Hands are clapped together, a clap

to every syllable, while repeating mantra four times.

4. Both turn around, women walking forwards, men backwards, clapping hands and speaking as in #3.
5. Now all face the line of direction (facing forward walking counterclockwise) walking with arms crossed and heads bowed.
6. Women again turn around as in #3. Hands are clapped while the arms remain crossed.
7. Both turn around, as in #4, clapping both hands, but with the arms crossed; always four times per cycle.
8. Now walk around each other going to the left, with left hands together four times, then to the right with right hands together four times.

HEBREW (JEWISH) SHALOM ALEICHEM DANCE

SHA-LOM A-LEI-CHEM SHA-LOM A-LEI-CHEM SHA-LOM — SHA-LOM— SHA-

LOM A-LEI-CHEM SHALOM A-LEI-CHEM SHA-LOM— SHA—LOM— SHA- LOM—

For six or more people. Count off: one, two, one, two, or may be done in couples, odd numbers (or women) move counterclockwise, even numbers (or

men) move clockwise: pairs face each other. Partners join hands, walk around each other, raising and lowering arms, singing "SHALOM ALEICHEM, SHALOM ALEICHEM" (Peace be with you) with arm movements. Partners then break apart and spin away from each other, arms raised up vertically, saying "SHALOM, SHALOM" spinning, each going in his assigned direction (clockwise or counterclockwise). Partners then re-join hands and repeat the phrases moving around each other and spinning in the opposite direction, arriving at a new partner.

Continue until a full round of the circle is completed, with each person greeting all those going in the opposite direction. If the group is small, dance may be continued longer.

DIVINE ATTRIBUTE DANCE WITH PARTNERS

The women form an inside circle and the men form a circle around them. The leader chooses a Divine Attribute, one of the Ninety-Nine Wazifas or Names of God. The women turn and take a partner. The Wazifa may be recited as the partners hold hands and circle each other to the right and then to the left. Or the partners can be instructed to greet each other with one of the gestures and Attributes given earlier. This practice helps people see Divinity in each other. Both circles advance to the next partner to the right.

ISLAM: KALAMA DANCE

LA IL LA HA EL IL LA HU
LA IL LA HA EL IL LA HU
LA IL LA HA EL IL LA HU
MOHAMMEDA RASSOUL LILLAH
MOHAMMEDA RASSOUL LILLAH

(There is no God but God, none exists save He, Mohammed is the Prophet of God) If possible, alternate men and women in circle, women to right. All join hands, moving backwards with hands down, saying or singing "LA IL LA HA." As this is a negative phrase, performers move backwards with hands down. Then they move forward singing "EL IL LA HU" raising their arms towards the center.

Then the man takes the right hand of the woman to his left. They sing "MOHAMMEDA RASSOUL LILLAH", moving around each other. Then he takes the left hand of the woman to his right. Then the man stands on the left of his new partner. A variation of this would be to have everyone drop hands and spin individually first to the right and then to the left on "MOHAMMEDA RASSOUL LILLAH."

(from Spiritual Dancing, compiled by Wali Ali)

LORD OF THE DANCE

Dance, dance wherever you may be,
For I am the Lord of the Dance, said He.
And I'll lead you all wherever you may be,
I'll lead you all in your dance, said He.

I danced on the day when the world was begun,
I danced in the moon and the stars and the sun,
I danced in the heavens and I came down to earth,
In Bethlehem I had my birth.

(Chorus)

134

I danced for the scribe and the pharisee,
But they wouldn't dance and they wouldn't
    follow me;
I danced for the fishermen James and John.
They came with me and the Dance went on.

(Chorus)

It was on the Sabbath that I cured the lame,
The "holy" people said it was a shame.
So they stripped and they whipped and they
    hung me on high,
And left me there on the cross to die.

(Chorus)

It was on a Friday that the sky turned black.
You know it's hard to dance with the devil on
    your back.
I leapt from my body and flew on high,
For I am the dance that can never ever die.

(Chorus)

They buried my body and they thought that
    I had gone,
But I am the Dance that goes on and on,
And I'll live in you if you will live in Me,
For I am the Lord of the Dance, said He.

Ancient Folksong, origin unknown.

BREATH

"The Breath is an absolute, profound, and pure way of communication from all planes of existence to other planes."

S.A.M.

"There is only one thing to be gained in life, and that is to remember God with each breath; and there is only one loss in life, and that is the breath drawn without the remembrance of God."

Abu Hashim Madani
(Murshid of Hazrat Inayat
Khan, Murshid's Murshid)

"A recent edition of the Wall Street Journal has a headline 'Man can control his automatic nervous system.' This newspaper superman yoga trick was taught to any and all who came to Murshid's house on Sunday nights. 'Take a long breath and be conscious you're taking a long breath,' he would say after asking everybody to just be conscious of your breath. 'Now take a short breath and just be conscious you're taking a short breath.' Then after several breaths, two or three only, he would instruct, 'Now take a heavy breath and be conscious you're taking a heavy breath,' and two or three or four breaths later, 'Now take a light breath and just be conscious you're taking a light breath.' After a pause he would say, 'Now refine that breath as fine as you can make it.' There would be no sound in the sound as breaths were refined. 'Now breathe in all the LOVE that you are capable of breathing in: love in and love out, love in and love out,' and then he'd do it. 'Alright, now breathe in all the JOY that you are capable of breathing out; joy in joy out, joy in and joy out.' And when that had been practiced for a few moments, moments only, he'd say 'Alright, now with the breath very refined breathe in all the PEACE that you can breathe in, and breathe out all the peace that you can breathe out; peace in, peace out.' This would be practiced. 'Now expand that peace to fill this room.' This would be practiced. 'Now expand that peace over the city,' etc. These were called the Jhanas of Lord Buddha."

Mansur

ON BREATH

1. Breath controls all aspects of life from the seen to the unseen. When breath is in the body life is in the body, and when breath is not in the body life is not in the body.

Ryazat (Esotericism): Take a thought, inhale, hold the thought. Exhale and try to hold the thought; there will be a difference. Thus we can learn there is an association between breath and thought, breath and life.

2. Breath may be called the essence of man from one point of view. As individual being, man is mind. As collective being, man is Adam. It was into Adam's nostrils that God breathed the breath of life. It is breath which invigorates each and all men. It is mind which makes the man; it is breath or spirit which unites men, which forms Adam. This makes possible the Brotherhood of Man in the Holy Spirit or Divine Breath.

3. One notices that after a rain the air is purified. This is one part of the process by which poisons are removed from the atmosphere, but it is only one part. . . .

4. Exhalation does not always remove all noxious gases. When it does not some poisons are left in the body. Therefore, disciples learn to breathe with the whole body and so control inhalation and exhalation.

5. Breath is not to be confused with air. It is something like the relation between magnetism and iron. There is magnetism apart from iron, that is, there is energy apart from matter. The energy connected with breath is called prana. The science of breath may be called pranavada in Sanskrit and Pasi Anfas in the Sufi language.

6. What are called spirit and matter in English correspond in some respects to what are called Shiva and Shakti in Sanskrit. The body, being the temple of the holy Spirit has accommodation for both Shiva and Shakti.

7. What is called the Neck Center in Indian esoterics corresponds more or less to the glottis in man. This organ or gland sends material into the digestive tract and spirit with air to the lungs. All functions in man are of the Shiva or Shakti varieties.

8. Ryazat:- Breathe identifying yourself with breath. Breathe holding Darood, i.e., "Toward the One," with each inhalation and exhalation. Identify yourself with the breath; identify with the Darood. This helps free you from identification with the body.

9. Practice meditation by repeating the Darood ("Toward the One") either a prescribed number of times or at least five minutes daily. Learn to feel the life-force entering the body. Identify yourself with the breath, identify yourself with the life-force. Do not identify yourself with the body. Thus you will learn to actualize: "This is not my body, this is the

temple of God." This is used as a disciplinary practice for beginners; it is used as a method of identification (fana or yoga) by the more advanced.

10. The degree of spiritual evolution can be measured by the breath — its power, its sweetness, its rhythm and its tonicity. Spirit and breath become one, and the grade of spiritual evolution is measured by the breath.

11. Every element in the breath attracts a similar element in another person's breath. This is one of the reasons for harmony between people. . . .

12. Every inhalation is God's gift to man and every exhalation is man's sacrifice to God. . . .

"WATCH YOUR BREATH"

"Murshid and I were out for a walk. We came to a busy street with six lanes of cars whizzing by in both directions. There was no stop sign. He said, 'Watch your breath!', and grabbed my hand and dragged me into the street. I felt like a wild stallion rearing on its hind legs and trying to get away. He kept shouting, 'Watch your breath!' The cars whizzed by on all sides. Needless to say, we made it across safely."

Fatima

13. Christ is born when breath enters man's body, and Christ is crucified when man thinks of himself.

Ryazat: Practice thinking of the breath; practice thinking of the breath with Darood; practice concentrating on Love; practice thinking of oneself. One will notice a great change. This self-thought is called Nafs by Sufis and is the greatest obstacle to life and happiness.

14. Breathing in unison helps bring harmony. Breathing with Darood helps increase that harmony. Breathing in Darood with a common concentration, e.g., the Sufi symbol, brings a still greater harmony.

Ryazat: Try each of these alone or with others and experience the results.

15. There is a difference in the breath of each kingdom: mineral, vegetable, animal and human.

Ryazat: Try concentrating in turn on a rock or mineral, a precious stone, grass, a tree, an insect and a four-legged animal. Notice the difference in your breathing; (this subject is continued in the commentary on the "Inner Life").

16. Disharmonies arise because of clashes in the rhythm of breath. These disharmonies can be removed by singing, dancing, devotion and esotericism. Therefore, Sufis use Wazifas and practice Zikars, not only to bring peace and harmony to each person, but also to each group.

17. Both inhalation and exhalation have an effect upon the atmosphere and it can be harmonious or inharmonious in relation to the atmosphere of

another. But when the etheric element is present, it destroys the nafs (ego-mind) and prevents inharmony. Esoteric practices regulate breathing.

18. Inhalation and exhalation affect and are affected by every form of thought, speech and action. The details of this are taught to Sufis in the science of Mysticism.

19. Life-force enters with the breath and leaves with the breath. This life-force is stored in the body. It is not the result of caloric intake through food. A stout man may obtain many calories from his food without being able to utilize them in actions. If the caloric theory alone were true, the stout would always be superior to the thin. The energy in an electric battery is derived from the chemicals introduced and not from the material of the battery. In a similar way the life-force vitalizes the body and the body utilizes the life-force. Therefore, the body is an accommodation and not a person.

20. Shiva is great-energy and Shakti is body material. In the Jewish mysticism there are these aspects expressed as Mi (meaning who) and Ma (meaning what). It is the interaction between Shiva and Shakti, between Mi and Ma which accounts for all of life.

21. In some Hindu philosophies such as Samkhya, one is disciplined to identify with Purusha (Shiva) and become free from Prakriti (Shakti). For this, mental instruction does not suffice. Esotericism (Ryazat) must be practiced.

22. The goddess Kali represents the divinisation of material forces apart from spirit. This can only be relatively true. There is no Purusha without a trace of Prakriti; there is no Prakriti without a trace of Purusha. The body is not entirely dead because of the absence of life-breath; it is then only an accommodation for subhuman forces.

23. Thus the breath makes the mortal out of the animal. Thus the breath makes the immortal out of the mortal.

24. The Sufi does not force any type of development or activate any gland or center. It is mastery and control of the breath which spiritualizes the whole personality. When the breath and bloodstream and mind are purified by yoga exercises and meditation, the flower of the heart and soul open through the combined efforts of the sun, rain, and earth within.

25. Purification may come through the repetition of sacred phrases. In Sufism Wazifas are so used.

26. Given a problem: Meditate on the problem. Given a problem, meditate on "Toward the One."
    Ryazat: Fikar-concentrate on La ilaha with each exhalation and on El il Allah with each inhalation. Do this 20, 33, or 101 times, according to the intensity of the problem. Now after this re-concentrate on the problem. There should be an influx of Kashf or insight that will help throw light on the problem, perhaps solve the problem. This is generally true of headaches, small pains and personal disturbances with loved ones.

27. Practice of Darood ("Toward the One") will generally give one more strength from another person. It is therefore not necessary to hold inimical thoughts. By these methods of practicing the presence of God one assures himself of self-firmness, and helps to build up with and from others. We all breathe the same atmosphere, and therefore are in communion whether we are aware of it or not.

28. Self-consciousness and self-thinking (manas) are the obstacles to knowledge. No doubt we must and should use our minds. But mental utilization apart from universal harmony is beneficial neither to oneself nor to the generality.

29. The Hindu repeats, "Neti, neti." The Sufi has the positive practices of Darood, Zikar and Fikar.

30. The small self is not overcome by any attention to the self. The small self becomes of even less importance in practicing the praise of God or repeating His Attributes.

31. The Praise of God is the RIGHT PATH. Then there is no room for ego. The ego is not effaced, but is transmuted by joining in the praise.

32. Inhalation and exhalation both have their sounds and also their colors. Each of these has its significance.

33. The movement of earth around the sun necessarily alters the metaphysical constitution of

the atmosphere. Motion of earth, angle of sun's declination, intensity of light or degree of darkness, all have their peculiar effects. Light has a direct action upon consciousness and so affects breath. . . .

34. In a purified body, the etheric element helps to clarify the tone and beautify the expression. Mild breathing brings about that condition of which Jesus spoke, "Blessed art the poor in spirit." Thus mild breathing may increase the scope for magnetism and bliss.

35. The breath sciences enable one to understand the Sufi mysticism in all its aspects.

36. If oxygen were the sole supporter of life one could breathe contentedly in an atmosphere of pure oxygen. But pure oxygen could also consume. Shiva is not only the divinity in life, he is the destroyer and transformer.

37. The earth itself breathes. The Mother requires prana for her life. Only deserts remain practically without it. After a rain the air is purified. No doubt this increases what the scientists call ozone. Ozone is not only physically activated oxygen, it is also a carrier for the all-pervading power in space. Yogis and ascetics often live in high mountain areas where there is less denseness and less oxygen, but where the ozone is comparatively higher.

38. An adept controlling his breath and able to draw the blessings of Nayaz can adapt himself to any environment.

NAYAZ

Beloved Lord, Almighty God!
Through the rays of the Sun,
Through the waves of the air,
Through the All-pervading Life in space,
Purify & revivify me, and I pray,
Heal my body, heart and soul.
Amen.

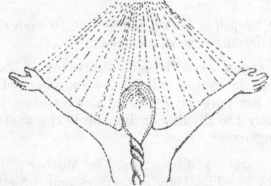

39. Nayaz proposes there are three ways toward health, viz.: through the rays of the sun, through the waves of the air, and through the all-pervading power in space. By space is meant asman or akash, which is the accommodation for all power. Both this power and the magnetisms contained in air enter the body through the channels of breath.

40. Breath is also light. It carries light, it carries color. It invigorates the whole body or any portion of it to which it is directed.

41. Concentrating on the heart, one can purify the breath. Concentrating on the breath and blowing "Hu" one can purify the heart.

42. The breath is the channel for many kinds of magnetism, and what is called baraka — which also means blessing. The Murshid blowing on the disciple can help and bless him. The Shifayat (healer) blowing on the patient can help him. The adept blowing on food and drink can help anybody.

43. Practice of Fikar with consciousness of breath develops what can be called the ark which carries the soul symbolically in the next world and carries the soul actually in all worlds.

44. Identifying oneself with breath is a form of self-effacement which takes one from mortality to immortality. Material things are left behind; spiritual "things" are carried to the next world — carry one to and through the next world.

45. All the denseness of earth is left behind when one has this breath realization.

"Once I had an injury at Kaaba Allah and the pain was intense and Pir-O-Murshid appeared and said, 'Don't grab your knee, grab your breath.' "

Diaries – May 23, 1963

Photo:Mansur

MEDITATION

"All the books in the world are not worth five minutes of meditation."

Diaries – March 26, 1965

EMPTY WAY / FULL WAY

It cannot be said that there is any monopoly on truth, and yet, until the appearance of Sufism, there was a negative approach to truth (the path of naughtness, nothingness) and a positive approach to truth (the path of Unity). By the negative approach we can include the way of quietism, monism, non-materialism, inaction, denial of self, denial of falsehood, and all the East Asiatic methods and schools based upon the passing into naughtness or emptiness and thence to fullness. There is Taoism, which has opposed self-expression and positivism; Hinduism, which has denied the reality of many (illusion) and sensual perception; Buddhism, which came to the denial of self and which has refused to recognize soul and finite gods. All these methods, however, lead to the same goal called Tao, Mukti, Nirvana, by the way of denial, from one to zero to infinity.

On the other hand, we find Moses, who preached the Unity of God, Jesus, who taught the way of Love, Zarathustra, who instructed people in practical arts and gave the message of Purity. These were positive paths to realization.

Although Mohammed in general followed the positive method of his predecessors, he taught "La illaha - el Allahu," (There is Nothing — but God), thus combining the negative and positive, and from him Sufism took its cue for a newer line of development.

"If you could perform a 'Meditation on Salat' you could develop some Wisdom. Take each line and use it, and then each name, and use it as a meditative subject for one month. . .

Personal Letter March 24, 1964

SALAT

Most Gracious Lord, Master, Messiah and Saviour of humanity,
We greet Thee with all humility.
Thou are the First Cause and the Last Effect,
the Divine Light and the Spirit of Guidance,
Alpha and Omega.
Thy Light is in all forms, Thy Love in all beings:
In a loving mother, in a kind father, in an innocent child,
In a helpful friend, in an inspiring teacher.
Allow us to recognize Thee in all Thy holy names and forms:
As Rama, as Krishna, as Shiva, as Buddha.

Let us know Thee as Abraham, as
Solomon, as Zarathustra,
As Moses, as Jesus, as Mohammed, and in
many other names and forms,
known and unknown to the world.
We adore Thy past, Thy presence deeply
enlightens our being.
and we look for Thy Blessing in the future.
O Messenger, Christ, Nabi, the Rassoul of
God,
Thou Whose heart constantly reaches
upward,
Thou comest on earth with a Message,
As a dove from above when dharma decays,
And speakest the Word that is put into
Thy mouth,
As the Light filleth the crescent moon.
Let the star of the Divine Light, shining in
Thy heart,
Be reflected in the hearts of Thy devotees.
May the Message of God reach far and
wide,
Illuminating and making the whole of
humanity as
One single Brotherhood, in the
Fatherhood of God.

Amen.

(The following three sections prepared by Wali Ali.)

MUJAHIDA MEDITATION

After the Prophet Mohammed and his followers had been successful in securing the Arabian peninsula from external enemies, so that they could practice their religion, he said, "We have been successful in the lesser holy war (Jihad) against external enemies, now it is time to take up the Greater holy war (Mujahida) against those enemies within our own selves, against hatred and jealousy and greed, etc." Murshid would often remark that the Kurekshetra, the battlefield upon which *The Bhagavad Gita* is spoken, is in truth the battlefield of the heart. It is with this kind of consciousness that the Mujahida meditation is undertaken.

One begins by simply watching the breath, gradually refining it and making it rhythmical throughout. Consciousness is focused on the heart center in the middle of the breast. You feel your breath gradually massaging and soothing this center of feeling. After doing this for a few minutes until it is a natural process with no mental strain, one moves to the next phase of meditation. One then internally looks into one's heart and feels the impressions (samskaras) that are lodged therein. There may be the surface impressions of the day, the mundane worries of one's existence. One notices and releases each and all of these; they are released by the gentle massaging action of the breath on the heart. As surface impressions are released, deeper impressions make themselves known. One may come face to face with a grudge against someone, with an impression of rejection and self-pity, with deeply ingrained emotions of fear or anger. Whatever impression comes up, you face it forthrightly, shining the light of your consciousness on it, continuing the massaging action of the breath (which may have the name ALLAH inhaled and exhaled on it). You may come upon impressions that resist your efforts; they have lain for so long in your heart that a rusting process has set in. Be assured that by patient effort and trust in Allah, even the most persistent impression can be released, if not in one meditation, then in one hundred and one perhaps. This process has been called polishing the Aladdin's Lamp of the heart.

An essential thing about this practice is that all external judgment is suspended. When the faults of friends and enemies well up as realities in one's inner vision, one looks for and finds the resonance of this fault in one's own being, the sympathetic vibration or impression in one's own heart. Then instead of trying to correct the person or situation on the outside, one gently and patiently massages and releases this impression inside oneself. The without is the same as the within. When this becomes conscious and the inner purification takes place, then the within becomes as the without, and this is the secret behind this meditation. For one finds that by working on the impression inside one's self with love and forthrightness, one actually helps purify the outward situation as well.

By the conclusion of this meditation, you should reach the state where your heart-being has become transparent, free from impressions, flooded with light, and in its natural condition which is love.

TOWARD THE ONE
(Darood)

The practice of breathing in and out the English phrase "Toward the One" can be done at almost any time. One should breathe in a most natural fashion without attempting to alter the breath in any way. You simply become one with your breath in whatever condition it may be in. The thought and feeling of oneness held in such a fashion allows a person to become united with whatever space or situation he finds himself in. Gradually the boundaries of one's being dissolve, so that external distractions are overcome by merging with them, including them in the overall compass of your being. This breath can be used (as in the papers on walk) when one is focused on a particular goal; in other words, you become one-pointed in your concentration. For example, driving a car you have the consciousness of a person driving a car; that and no side trips.

CONCENTRATION ON SYMBOLS

There are two things to be gained from such a practice. We can achieve one-pointedness of mind by learning to keep our glance and thought entirely focused, without wavering, for increased periods of time. This disciplined attention will serve us well in all activities of life. The second thing is that by interesting ourselves in an object of concentration, we begin to assimilate the essence of that object into our own being. What we concentrate upon, we become.

The symbol used should be made for visual simplicity. We begin by sitting at a comfortable distance with the drawn or constructed symbol at eye level. Breathing rhythmically, we concentrate on that symbol, resisting the tendencies of the mind to wander. Our attention should be totally absorbed in the object of concentration; when the mind wanders we simply bring our attention time and again back to the object. No judgment. Do this for five minutes with the eyes open. A more advanced phase of this same practice is to follow this with another five minutes of holding the symbol (with eyes closed, in one's inner vision) clearly and definitely, without wavering. It may take much continued practice before one is able to do such concentrations properly.

The following symbols are given for beginning work in this area:

1) the equilateral triangle (point upwards)
2) the heart
3) the dove
4) the circle with a dot in the middle
5) Sufi symbol of winged heart

Continued practice with any of these symbols should lead to an inner realization of their real meaning.

Photo: William B. Giles

GATHAS
OF THE
DHARMA

GATHAS
OF THE DHARMA

It was during his travels in Asia (in 1956 and 1961) that Sam received the recognition and final training he required to teach in the West. His Buddhist realization was confirmed by Nyogen Senzaki (who wrote *Zen Flesh, Zen Bones*) whom Murshid referred to as "old fatso." A step-by-step description of the perfection of the Hinayana and Mahayana Buddhist paths, it is a map and an introduction to the *Mahamudra*.

"This is the doctrine of No-Doctrine
Which brings Peace to heart and mind."
Stanza 2

1

THE DOCTRINE OF
NO-DOCTRINE

Bhagavat,

let me lay this down
And stop this ceaseless
coming and going;
O Bhagavat, I want no
heavenly crown
Nor diamond palace without that life bestowing.
The sutras read, the fruits are set aside,
And heart is kept in steady meditation;
The ocean's roar is gone and I abide
At rest, beyond all conscious limitation.
The doctrine of No-Doctrine teaches that Peace
    that is not-Peace
War is two and Peace is one.
When another says, there are two opinions,
When there are two opinions, there is strife,
    there is division, there is bitterness.
From bitterness comes the utterance of self,
    which is war.

2

Not by shadow is light known but
   by its substance,
Not by reflection is color known but
   by its essence,
Not by impression is mind known but
   by its Buddha nature,
Not by words is Truth known but by its Being.
There is no word that was lost.
Every word is lost, every philosophy is false,
Yet from Suchness comes every word
   and every teaching:
This is the doctrine of No-Doctrine
Which brings Peace to heart and mind.

3
THE UNWEAVING OF SELF

Go on the first adventure, go on the second
   adventure, go on the third adventure!
The first adventure leads through restraint
   of physical desire to emancipation;
The second adventure leads through
   right-mind-control to enlightenment;
The third adventure leads through highest
   concentration of spirit to tranquilization.
The first adventure betrays the Dharma,
The second adventure betrays the Abidharma,
The third adventure betrays the Saddharma.

Who knows Nirmanakaya, Sambhogakaya and
Dharmakaya
To be One in essence,
He has completed the adventure though
he start not.
These are the adventures of the unweaving of self,
The clothing is turned to cloth and the
cloth to skein,
The skein is returned to its original source.

4
BEGINNING OF THE FIRST ADVENTURE
RIGHT IDEAS

This is the first adventure,
It is the adventure of the Here-Now,
It is composed of eight stages:
Right Ideas, Right Resolution, Right Speech,
Right Behavior, Right Vocation, Right Effort,
Right Mindfulness, and Right Concentration.
By ideas are forms made, by ideas are forms
destroyed.
What is the mind with pure ideas?
What is the mind with no ideas?
Free from karma, free from sin, free from self,
Mind may hold ideas, mind may restrain ideas.
The essence of Right Ideation is the doctrine
of No-Doctrine.

5
RIGHT RESOLUTION

The second stage is not different from
   the first stage:
As the crystal splits the light-ray into colors,
So is the Path of Deliverance regarded
   as Eight-fold;
Eight-fold yet One-fold is the Path of Deliverance.
Right Resolution leads to termination of karma.
Who so, unwavering, controls the mind-waves,
He is the Peace-maker, the Gina, there is no other.

6
RIGHT SPEECH

The third stage of the first adventure
   is Right Speech.
Thought controlled by Will is the key
   to Right Speech.
To say, "This is," is not Right Speech,
Neither to say, "This is not," belongs
   to Right Speech.
Abandon word-shadows, this is the first counsel.

7

RIGHT BEHAVIOR

*W*hat is Right Behavior?
Know Right Behavior not as antithesis
    to "wrong behavior."
That which is good is the shadow of light,
That which is evil is the shadow of shadow.
Action in harmony with Dharma, this
    is Right Behavior;
Action entirely free from Karma, this
    is Right Behavior.
All sentient beings contain enlightenment,
Know Buddhahood to be the Omnipresent Essence.

8
RIGHT VOCATION

*S*eeking neither gold nor glory nor power,
Performing work in accordance with
    highest principles,
Removing the shadow of self in all activities,
Preserving perfect freedom and guided by
    the highest wisdom,
One attains deliverance:
Such is the purpose of Right Vocation.

9
RIGHT EFFORT

Know Right Effort not to be effort toward
  some particular end,
Know it only as Right Effort which
  delivers from suffering;
To encourage zeal in oneself,
To see oneself in all forms,
This is Right Effort.

10
RIGHT MINDFULNESS

Thought in accordance with Dharma,
Speech in accord with Dharma,
Action in accord with Dharma,
These are of the essence of Right-Mindfulness.
When self is laid aside,
When thought casts no more and grasps no more,
This brings emancipation through
Right-Mindfulness.

11
RIGHT CONCENTRATION

Know the eighth state of the First Adventure to be
  none other than the other stages
  of the First Adventure.
When these seven stages are as one stage,

This is the condition of Right Concentration.
Excluding shadow-thoughts,
Ceasing to reflect on shadow-words
    and action-shadows,
Purifying the Universal Spirit called breath,
In Allness is found the perfect Peace.

12

BEGINNING OF THE SECOND ADVENTURE
THE FLOWER

This is the Second Adventure,
The adventure of Now, but not Here,
The epitome of the eight-fold First Adventure.
Always the First Adventure:
The Second is the flower of its seed,
    the Third is the perfume of its flowers;
Behind the golden hills of Sukhavati,
Heralds a new dawn.
The birds are singing and myriad fountains
    play in splendid light.
Peace will come when there is no thought of Peace.

13

FIRM MIND

The second stage of the second adventure is
    not to be considered
Separate from the first stage of the
    second adventure.

165

Know this stage to be the Right Resolution
    of the Firm Mind.
What is the Firm Mind:
It transcends discrimination and thought,
It discriminates truly,
It thinks truly.
What is it that thinks?
This is the Buddha-mind, free from the
    distinctions and differences of man.
The clear lamp brightens the hall of the temple,
Flowers decorate the altar.

14
RIGHT WORDS

Namo Amida Butsu explains itself
Conception free from concepts,
Resolution free from thoughts,
Speech undetermined by words,
This is the Right Use of Words which leads
    to emancipation.

15
RIGHT CONDUCT

The fourth stage of the Second Adventure
    is Right Conduct.
When effort distinguishes neither self nor not-self,
This is the Golden Rule of the Golden Path.

16
RIGHT LIVELIHOOD

The fifth stage of the Second Adventure
　　is Right Livelihood.
Know this Right Livelihood to be the
　　conduct of Sramanas;
He is not a Sramana who, giving up the world,
　　attaches thought to it;
Not by shaved head and begging bowl is one
　　a Sramana,
But by detachment from objects of sense is
　　one a Sramana.

17
RIGHT EFFORT

In objects of sense the mind of the purified one
　　sees the Buddha-nature reflected,
But the mind of the purified one is not dependent
　　upon objects of sense.
Casting ambition aside, ceasing to strive,
Throwing away all burdens,
The consciousness is freed from the bondage
　　of the elements.
This secures emancipation through Right Effort.

18
MINDFULNESS OF SPIRIT

The seventh stage of the Second Adventure
　　is Right Mindfulness,

This is Right Mindfulness of the Spirit;
When, by holding back, one expresses,
When by holding back, one delivers the
    perfume of Dharma,
This is Right Mindfulness.

19
SAMADHI

*t*his is the eighth stage of the glorious
    Second Adventure.
It is not to be considered apart from all other
    stages of the Second Adventure;
It is not to be considered apart from any stage
    of the First Adventure.
This is Right Concentration.
What is Samadhi?
Definition defines, segregates, distinguishes;
Samadhi integrates, unites, amalgamates.
The coal mine is not a light house,
Nor is the clod a lantern,
Definition of Samadhi is not Samadhi,
Description of Samadhi is not Samadhi.
Words are no more.

20
BEGINNING OF THE THIRD ADVENTURE

*t*his is the first stage of the Third Most
    Glorious Adventure;

168

This is the adventure of the not-here and not-now,
And the not not-here and not not-now.
This is the knowledge of Dharmakaya through
    Right Intuition.
Earth was, then rocks and stones;
Sky was, then planets and stars;
Suchness was, is, will be, will be being,
    was being.

21
PEACE

What is the mystery of incarnation?
What incarnates and why?
The answer is: "Cease to question."
By questioning, a shadow is thrown over truth.
Look at the sun ten minutes with the shades drawn
And your face toward the wall.
What are the proper vows for the advocate of
    Peace?
Cease to advocate, that is Peace.
This is the second aspect of the Path's fulfillment
On the Third Most Glorious Adventure.

22
RADIATION

Right Radiation is Right Behavior with
    ego removed,
Let light shine before men that they may learn,

That they may rejoice.
Mind calm, serene, poised, indifferent,
Radiates pure essence through
   multifarious attribution.
This is called the third aspect of the Third
   Most Glorious Adventure.

23
LOVE

*t*his is the grand mystery of the fourth stage
   of the Third Most Glorious Adventure:
Dharmakaya puts an end to all admonition;
"No adultery" — this is the admonition
   to the ignorant,
"Love all" — this is the resolution
   of the Sramana;
In the perfect union of Dharmakaya there is
   the death of senseless words.

24
RIGHT ENVIRONMENT

Let the enlightened live among mountains —
Which is the Right Environment for the sage?
Dharmakaya is environment,
This is not time, This is not space; This is
   not conditioned existence.
Do not go, do not come, do not enter, do not leave.
What is the Right Environment for meditation?
In the midst of Conditioned Existence,
From the midst of Conditioned Existence,

Having no relation to Conditioned Existence.
This is the fifth stage of the Glorious
   Third Adventure.

25

HEART

*t*hrough Right Mindfulness
Does Dharmakaya touch all atoms of mind and body;
When the sun rises the cock ceases.
No more unsubstantiality,
No more delusive movements of consciousness.
Here now touches itself.
This is the seventh stage of the Third Most
   Glorious Adventure.

26

NIRVANA

*t*he sun casts shadows and the earth emits light,
The worm is the teacher, the Sramana
   is the scholar.
Babies discipline their grandfathers,
And handkerchiefs are used for laughter;
With closed eyes is toil accomplished,
And in the daylight is great sloth.
Until Nirvana is surrendered, Nirvana
   is not gained.
This is called the eighth stage of the Third
   Most Glorious Adventure;
So is It called,
But until there is no calling, It is not.

27

PERFECTION

*t*hus do I hear:
The Tathagata is not absent from the earth,
The Tathagata is not absent from the minds of men,
Neither from the Paradise of Sukhavati
Nor from the paradises above or below,
Nor from the hearts of sentient beings —
From none is the Perfect One absent.
Neither is the Tathagata missing in Hell,
Nor is his presence wanting in Avichi;
From no point of time nor area of space is
    the Enlightened One gone.
Neither from conception nor deception
    is he missing.
What is Nirvana?
Restraint from definition, restraint
    from dissimulation,
Freedom from distinction, unshackled by ties
    of limitation,
This is but the accompaniment to the Song of Peace,
A song not sung in words but by the
    Breath of Compassion,
Breathing joy and mercy,
One is what one becomes
And there are not two.

KARUNA YOGA GITA

(The Song of Compassion)

The musical quality of his poetry is perhaps best shown in *The Karuna Yoga Gita*, "The Song of Compassion," which is actually a manual of instruction for Heart Meditation. Sam was closely connected to the Chisti Sufis, who are known for teaching through their music and poetry.

Hail to the Sadguru!
Who brings all manner of
    blessings to the world,
Who absorbs its poisons and
    revivifies it,
Who carries the torch of Dharma,
Who exemplifies perfection for
    striving humanity,
Who comes to sanctify and
    rebuild.

Love, love, love beyond love,
Heart-beating, heart-moving,
    pulsating love;
Light, light, light beyond light,
Outstretching, outpouring,
    infinite light;
Life, life, eternal life,
Creating, preserving,
    assimilating life.
And so it was,
And so it is,
And so it will be,
Forever then, forever now,

forever thence,
The love sought love,
The light sought light,
The life sought life,
So the world came into being.
Then man stepped forth, created in the
    Divine Image,
In the Image and Likeness of the One-All-Only.

Hail to man, supreme above created beings!
Hail to man, paramount to every institution!
Hail to man, superior even to the unseen!
Hail to man, may he ever be blessed!
This is the book of Absorption-through-love,
The Karuna Yoga Gita,
Whereby with the opening of heart
The heart can regain heart,
Man comes face to face with his Creator,
The soul finds its eternal resting-place,
And the purpose of existence is revealed.
This is the Karuna Yoga Gita,
The Song of all songs,
Endless and powerful, yet gentle and tender,
Pouring forth and in and through every heart,
Heart seeking heart — let us seek what we may
    find.

Within the secret confines of the heart
There lies the sacred door;

This is the manger wherein Christ was born,
Who said, "Seek and ye shall find,
Knock and it shall be opened unto you."
What shall we seek? Whither shall we find?
"Lo, the kingdom of the heavens is within you,"
In the very centre of the heart abides the key.

Lesson the first: THE MEDITATION OF THE HEART.

This meditation is a difficult task:
For it is not of the body, neither is it
   of the mind.
It is not associated with chakra-concentration.
It has nothing to do with complexities
   of any school.
It is not like any process in intellectualization.
Its very simplicity is its difficulty.
This meditation is a simple task:
There is nothing about it that a child cannot do.
Indeed by becoming as little children we
   may be more successful.
The heart is heart and nothing else,
Yet it is more than flesh, even more than feeling.

The Master has always said, "Thus,"
Whereupon the disciples have said:
"Thus-and-thus,"
Including their doctrines concerning the Master
    with the teachings of the Master;
In every time, in every place have teachings
    and doctrines conflicted,
So there has been turmoil, tribulation, warfare —
So many doctrines, each opposing the others,
    all opposing the teachings.
When shall we turn? When shall we return
    to the heart?
When shall we resume the teachings and
    discard the doctrines?
Let us turn, in silence let us turn to the heart,
Let us seek the secret asylum of the heart,
For therein lies the city of refuge,
    great beyond conception,
There is repose, there is salvation.
Seated in quiet comfort,
Laying aside woes and cares and problems,
Placing thoughts outside of consciousness,
Raising consciousness above thought,
Feel the love that emanates from the
    sun-centre of the heart.
Feel this love, find this love, follow this love —
That is all, that is the simplicity,
The ever-so-easy meditation of the heart.
Thus the baptism in the bosom of Christ,

This is *tauba,* this is *shuvo*, this is repentance,
This is the Way toward Love.

Lesson the second: THE CONCENTRATION OF
THE HEART

Practice not the Concentration until there is
progress in Meditation;
Therefore is there need for the Teacher to mark
one's footsteps.
In the schools for the young where the many attend,
The pupils do not mark their own papers,
the teachers do this;
But in the school of life, where only the few
even enter,
Many of those few would mark their own progress.
By their individual egos would they grade
themselves,
Becoming thus more tied to karma than even those
who do not enter —
If thou would judge thyself, come not even
into this school,
Remain at the threshhold or even stay away;
It will be better for thee.

Seated again in heart-repose as in Meditation,
Concentrate all faculties upon the form

of the heart;
Consider that this form is but the externality
    of the essence,
That essence and form are not two,
That essence and form are unseparate.
Utilize the sense of sight together with the
    faculty of thought,
Do not discard effort or imagination,
But bind all faculties by the feeling,
Feel and feel, and look with the heart-beat.
Therefore the Meditation is needed first, and
    afterwards the Concentration.

When the mind has been sufficiently impressed,
Hold the image within,
Let the thought hold the image,
Let the image inspire the thought,
Let the feeling dominate both thought
    and imagination.
Only when the feeling controls will
    the interest remain,
Only when the heart is master will
    the will-power operate,
Then step by step is consciousness elevated,
Then does the healing balm of heart
    purify the body,
Then does the vital energy of heart
    sanctify the body,
Then does the life of heart permeate the mind.
This is the baptism by blood,

For without thought is the blood elevated;
This is an elevation when there is no
attention to elevation,
This is a healing when there is no
consideration of healing,
This is a revitalization when there is no
consciousness of revitalization.

Keeping away all thoughts of self,
Maintaining fast the act with no ideas
of fruits-of-action,
Pursuing inward unity with steadfastness,
The heart begins to ebb and flow, to flow and ebb,
Love seeking love, light seeking light,
life seeking life.

What was this image that I saw before me?
I am the image, I am the form, I am the seer.

Lesson the third: BREATH AS THE WAY.

Hearken not to the ignorant who make mysteries
of the unknown,
And by their mystification keep seekers
from the door.
Every school has taught it from the most
ancient times,

And the Way to God is the Way to God,
    not man-thought-created.
By the blood and also by "spirit" shall we
    be baptized;
Alas for those foolish ignorant who separate
    blood from love,
Who oversimplify breath and overcomplicate spirit!
Alas, that the doctrines have overwhelmed
    the teachings
In all ages, in all parts of the world,
    leading to confusion!

The incoming breath is bliss,
The outgoing breath is serenity,
Serenity and bliss, bliss and serenity,
    out and in, in and out.
When the breath comes in massive waves,
    irregular, tempestuous,
Then is the life irregular, tempestuous,
    uncontrolled.
When the breath comes smooth, even,
    rhythmical,
Then is there life, then is potentiality;
But beware of the evenness of weakness,
Steer far from potentiality without vitality,
For such a breath is short and does not
    reach the inwards:
The inwards of the body it does not reach,
The inwards of the mind it does not touch,
It never arrives at the threshhold of heart.

"With difficulty comes ease" says Quran;
   so be it.
Therefore the rhythm is needed first,
Rhythm, smoothness, tranquillity,
And after that may the breath be lengthened,
And when it is lengthened it is strengthened.
But do this with the advice and counsel
   of the Guru,
Do not do this of self; do not experiment.
Dangerous as it is to experiment teacherless
   in the laboratory,
Multifold is the danger of self-experimentation;
Yet in water, in breath, in blood lay the
   mysteries of life.
(How we ignore the teachings even in
   proportion to revering the texts!)

When Meditation is practiced, calmness
   comes with ease;
When Concentration is performed, strength
   comes with facility.
So first the Meditation and the Concentration,
   then the Breath,
Yet each assists, each accommodates the others,
Each are sign-posts, guides on the Way,
Yet the Way is the Truth, the Way is the Life.
Blessed is he who comes by water, by blood
   and by breath. AMEN.

Lesson the fourth: THE CONTEMPLATION OF
THE HEART.

*W*hen the three lessons have been learned,
Then Contemplation may be tried,
But until the three lessons have been mastered
   at least in part,
Every effort at Contemplation will wipe away
   what has been achieved,
For to him that hath shall be given,
But from him that hath not shall be taken
   even that which he hath.
The Contemplation of the Heart is an
   activity of egolessness,
It is not by the ego that Contemplation is
   performed,
It is a performance without the ego,
So until the ego is subjected it is to be avoided.

*W*hen the three lessons have been learned,
   at least in part,
And when the teacher has requested,
Then is Contemplation to be practiced.
Seated in the same manner as in Meditation
   and Concentration,
Secure in the control of the penetrating, even,
   rhythmic breath,
One begins as in Concentration and
   then reverses it,
For instead of identifying self with ego

and seeking heart,
One identifies oneself with heart and seeks ego —.
Thus it is that one arrives at egolessness, not-self.
By the not-self, through the nonself
    contemplate heart-of-self,
Looking from outward in, no longer from inward out,
The Contemplation is the Concentration-in-reverse,
This is the first step in Contemplation.

In Meditation and Concentration self is and
    God is sought,
In Contemplation God is and self is sought.
Only by a psychological feat of egolessness
    can the non-ego be realized;
The philosophy of non-ego otherwise is verbal,
The philosophy of non-ego otherwise is vanity.
How many there are who preach of non-ego!
How many who go through a vain and useless
    non-violence!
The true Contemplation is the true non-violence,
The accommodation for an ever-expanding life,
Not a retreat from life, not a refuge from effort.
By effort is attainment achieved,
By the true effort resulting from the union of
    ego and non-ego,
But first one must strive on the path of non-ego,
Even as one has hitherto striven on the path of ego.
One must dissociate oneself from ego to progress,
Yet one must also look with compassion upon the

ego to progress;
This is the mystery, this is the purpose
of Contemplation,
Wherein the heart seeks heart, even seeks
the heart-of-self.

Lesson the fifth: THE EXPANSION OF HEART-CONSCIOUSNESS

*t*he expansion of heart-consciousness is not
to be essayed
Until Contemplation is practiced and
progress achieved;
Therefore do nothing without the Guru.
Unless there is love for the Guru there will be
no heart-expansion,
Unless there is love for the Guru there will only
be emotional intensification,
How many have identified emotional
intensification with love,
Only that on the morrow they identify it with hate!
Emotional intensification is a state of ego,
Wherein one is still bound, even more bound to
the Wheel-of-life-and-death,
And it is from this Wheel-of-life-and-death

that we seek deliverance.
If there is still emotional intensification,
One should concentrate upon the dot and circle,
One should follow the expansion and
    contraction of the breath,
One should feel oneself as nothing and as all —
This is a link in severance, this is a step
    toward liberty.
So long as the self is bound to self it is
    in bondage,
But the denial of self and of bondage only
    increases the bonds
And leads one deeper and deeper into the mire
    of delusion.
Effort without reverence is a waste of vitality,
Effort without reverence is a road to the crown
    of uselessness,
Effort without reverence destroys the
    psychic substance,
Effort without reverence only increases the
    toil of true effort.
Looking upon oneself from the without inwardly,
And from the inward outwardly,
Produce the realization of limitation
Whence expansion and growth are possible.
Feel the heart, find the pin-point
    within the heart,
Then grow with that pin-point on, and on,
    and on. . . .

There is no limit to this growth,
There is no end to this achievement,
Until the other shore is reached.

Love is not a word,
Love is not a thought,
Love is not a series of changing emotions —
However it be expressed,
In whatever modes it manifest,
 Love is the way to greatness, to life,
  to salvation.

Have pity on those who stop at faith and never
 arrive at love,
Have sorrow for those who revel in faith and
 never manifest love,
Have compassion for those who accentuate faith
 and never exercise love;
Who never knew the Master's mind,
Who never dream of the Master's heart,
Who never see the Master face-to-face.

Lesson the sixth: UNION OF SELF
AND NON-SELF
When one has advanced in Meditation,

When one has become skillful in Concentration,
When the breath ebbs and flows smoothly
   and rhythmically,
When there is serenity, when there is bliss,
When the heart feels the love of the Guru,
When Contemplation becomes the norm
   of the devotee,
And the heart-sway is expanded while
   mastery is retained,
Then it is possible to bring about the
   union of self-and non-self.
If one has not accomplished these things,
There is a return to egoicity,
Which is to be avoided above all things,
For it brings a return to samsara,
And adds to the world-store of unwholesome karma.

*W*hen there is humility and lack of ostentation,
Then it is possible to bring about union of
   self and non-self.
For, with the expulsion of breath one supposes:
"Now I am not, verily I am not, *neti, neti!*"
With the indrawing of breath one supposes,
"Now I am, verily I am, *ani, ani!*"
I am, I am not, *neti, ani,*
So the exhalation, so the inhalation,
So the denial, so the affirmation.
But as a pendulum cannot swing in
   one direction only,
So the consciousness cannot swing.

For if there is denial only death ensues,
And if there is assertion only
    death-in-life ensues,
So that one does not attain to mastery.
For the death-in-life is the sin or karma,
And the death-in-death is the final enemy,
So has the teaching gone, verily so has it been.
But the teaching is not without the actualization,
So the breath must be controlled,
Then as there are two sides to a coin,
    but one coin,
As there is swing and counter-swing
    to the pendulum,
So with the two aspects of breath:
Exhalation, inhalation - but a single breath-span.

Now from this singleness of breath
Realizing the two facets of one process,
Whereupon the breath joins man to God,
The breath brings God to man.
Now from this singleness of heart
Realizing self and non-self as undifferentiated,
Different in the world of manifestation,
Unseparate in the universal life-in-God.
Seek and ye shall find; verily if ye seek,
    shall ye find.

Lesson the seventh: COMPASSION.

*T*he union is not a blind event devoid of life,
The union is a complete event abundant with life;
The union is not a theoretical happening,
The union is that rebirth from within of which
    sages speak;
The union is an expansion of consciousness
    transcending limitation,
The union brings light, the union brings life,
    the union is love.

*O*h, for that marvelous love
    beyond intellectualization,
Which makes of this very universe a sport,
Which makes the greatest of the happenings of
    earth,
Yet overlooks not the smallest suffering
    of the least;
Whether the meek inherit earth or not, they
    inherit the heavens;
Whether the peacemakers are blessed on earth or
    not, they are above,
And the blessings become realities,
Not words or images or thoughts or ideals,
Verily are they real, truly are they supremely real.

*W*hen the love is fixed upon self, it is
    degraded toward pity;
When the love is fixed upon non-self, it is
    lost in passion,
Yet pity is a shadow of compassion,

And passion also is the umbra of compassion.
Not by Meditation or Concentration is
   compassion realized,
But by the ever-expanding heart,
Trained in the ways of love through
   devotion to the Guru,
Marked in the ways of love by the
   stimulation of the Guru,
Skilled in the ways of love through
   constant practices.
There is no theory of universal attitude,
There is either a complete view or its absence,
Not pretended but exhibited by one's every deed,
For the earth-born are veiled by their very egos,
While the twice-born are no longer veiled,
No longer see through a glass darkly, but
   now face-to-face.
With the expansion of the heart comes Compassion,
And with Compassion comes increased
   expansibility of heart,
That thereupon man becomes a Bodhisattva —
He is the vessel of heaven in the bowels of earth,
He incarnates God-in-man through his
   change of status.

Oh, the blessed Guru who makes this possible!
Oh, the wonderful Guru who bestows his gifts to us!
Producing happiness even here on earth,
Through the sublimation of self after
   union with non-self,

Whereupon the expanded consciousness full of light
Extends its sway of Mercy and Compassion,
Becomes free from the toils of lust and
    greed and temper,
And rises full-fledged like an image
    from the chrysalis.

Lesson the eighth: BODHISATTVA.

*W*hat we shall be, that we are;
Time is a bewitching delusion
    weaving enchantments,
Each enchantment unveiling the past but
    secluding the future,
All standing like gossamer webs over reality.
O soul, let me see your face!
Ask it of the stars whose light shines eons
    after they are not —
So true light shines for eons before it is,
For what it is is nothing before the seeing eye.
No man can see God, and live,
But dying-to-self becomes reality.
When heart is filled with compassion,
The deeper consciousness becomes aware of all;

Then man can say, "I am."
To another he cannot say, "I am not thou,"
For his "I am" is his "Thou art,"
And the veil of the temple has been rent.
Where would the light of the stars if
    the sun were not?
Where would the light of the eyes if
    the soul were not?
When these are, we are:
Then our beating sun-hearts pour forth compassion,
Pour forth love, pour forth mercy,
    pour forth blessing.
What is the aim of Karuna Yoga?
It is this, it is nothing but this.
The deep music of Reality pours
    through consciousness,
The deep light of Reality produces the
Nirmanakaya,
The body where matter and spirit meet,
Wedded by the eternal cohesion of
    dense and ethereal;
The abysmal and the hyperbolic are no longer apart,
Time is no more.

Avalokitesvara, need I look to thee?
Manjusri, art thou but mind enfoldment?
O the beating heart that feels all beating hearts!
O the sorrowing heart that knows
    all suffering hearts!
O the living heart that quickens

all quivering hearts!
This and the other beating hearts
   maintain the universe,
By them alone is karma squelched,
By them alone is the underlying
   truth made manifest,
The undying fire recreates fuel from the ashes,
The living waters of the cosmic flood are ebbing
And man becomes his own exemplary and savior —
Not in what he says or teaches,
But what he is.

Lesson the ninth: KARUNA YOGA.

Hail to the Guru, Self of my self.
Whose body was different, whose mind
   was delineate,
Whose heart I have become.
To me ever attached to him
I become his him-in-me and me-in-him, Svah!

When the effort passing step by step,
Experiencing stages, recognizing states,
Becomes so filled with love and
   light and compassion,

Then it recognizes this love and light
   and compassion on every side,
And there is nothing to which one is unattached.
When the love transcending self recognizes
   self no longer,
When the compassion transcending self feels
   equally the pain of all,
When the mercy transcending self sends
   blessing and healing everywhere,
When self becomes love and there is nothing
   left to love. . .
O that transforming wonder of redeeming light!
O that bliss of transcendental bathing!
O that wondrous calm of the life of life!
When time is gone and bodies are no longer,
The dark night of sleep is ended,
The dark sleep of night is gone;
The eye perceiving pierces all veils
And only suffering is dead.

*A*rise, awakened one, the Buddha-fields
   surround thee,
Thou art Christ and thou alone;
The history and the deed have run their course,
The mystery and the travail have been ended,
God among gods, yet a man of men,
The Great Work lays before thee.

*W*hat I was I am no longer,
What I was, not that have I become,

Until the I becomes a lie and the was-not is.
Canst thou by taking thought add to the hairs
of thy head?
O faith of heart and heart of faith,
Crown thou art now through faith and hope
to boundless love,
To boundless bliss, to boundless
understanding and wisdom,
Who can teach thee now who surpasseth all!
A little child, a hoary sage, a supernal being —
The shiny dewdrop has entered the Great Sea.

Lesson the Tenth HIERARCHY

*h*ail to the marvellous brotherhood
of wonder-workers!
Hearts linked to hearts to homogenize the universe,
Ladders from heaven to earth and earth to heaven,
Pulsations in the mystic, cosmic heart,
Ones in all and alls in one are they.

*g*o, adventurous one,
And when thou hast accomplished thy mission,
When thou hast fulfilled the purpose of

thine outer life,
When thou also hast experienced states and states,
When Meditation is thy wont
And Contemplation is thy constant habit,
When all the love and mercy blossom in thee,
Link thee to the before-and-after,
Err not in recognizing only those before thee,
Neither be thou deluded in blind evolution
Which falsely pictures perfection in the future.
The day is come and the day is now
And the day is naught but revelation of thy spirit,
And night thy sleep.
Thou art joined with thy brethren
Whose Khalif thou art there in thine unfoldment,
Behold the group of men and women acting as a
unit!
A stream of living lights connected with one
    central power station,
Unseparate, drawing from one unlimited
    unadulterated pool,
Unseparate, sending forth beneficence,
Unseparate in essence, heart beating with heart,
But whose rhythms are all for each and
    each for all,
When the earth in dark travail looks for help,
    thou art there;
When mothers bereaved and fathers wander
aimlessly,
    thou comest;

When the orphans look for guidance and affection,
  who else manifests?

Who can conceive the Universal Adam!
Who can comprehend the single Grand Man!
Those who know, who have given up without
  thought of reward;
Those who understand, who give because it
  is their nature,
Those who love, and loving, pour forth radiance;
These are the Sons and Daughters of God —
Not in the past, not in the future, evermore now:
These are the Messiahs of Humanity.

Lesson the eleventh: PERFECTION.

O song of songs beginning and ending
  in stillness!
O light of lights drawing from the abyss!
O Karuna Yoga which joins and joins not.
For joining and separation alike are illusions,
When there is realization that Naught else is,
When there is recognization that Naught else was,
When there is the supertranscendent perception —

This is it! Aye, this is it!
Carry on, O song of love, into that symphony!
Carry on, heart of heart, into that love!
Let me be enveloped in that glory
And let that glory manifest through me.
Here, body, lay thyself down;
Here, mind, give thyself up;
Here, heart, let thyself go!
For what art thou, o body, without thy Maker!
And what art thou, o mind, without thy Preserver!
And what art thou, o heart, without thy Essence!
Go, words into the Word of Wisdom!
Go, thoughts, into the stream of Intelligence!
Naught else was,
Naught else is,
Naught shall ever be, can ever be.
I die, and dying live evermore;
My sepulchre is light, my grave is glorification;
My resurrection is my very self.
Let this light shine ever in me and before me;
Let there be nothing which is without this light.
Fill the interstices, make straight
   the crooked paths,
Level the mountains, upraise the depths,
And let divine blessings flow ever
   through my person.
Before the all am I nothing —
But before the nothing am I all.

hail to thee, o Guru of Gurus,
The man-in-God and God-heart in humanity!
Thou art come to make this possible!
Thou art gone to enlighten grievous burdens!
Thou art here when no one is aware!
Thou art not when people say they see thee!
Hail to thee, God-incarnated-Saviour!
Hail to thee, very man of very humanity!
Aum!
          Svah!
                    Shanti!

                              Samuel L. Lewis

NYOGEN SENZAKI

SUFI BARKAT ALI

PAPA RAMDAS

MOTHER KRISHNABAI

HAZRAT INAYAT KHAN

Photo:Mansur

SUFI VISION &
INITIATION

"Sufi Vision and Initiation" is, in Sam's words, "a living testimonial of a Sufi who has passed the tests." It combines two term papers he wrote for extension courses he took in 1966. One paper, entitled "Genuine Versus Pseudo-Mystical Experience", received this remark from the teacher: "Would be an insult to give you a grade. But for the sake of the records: An 'A'." The other paper, "Vision and Ritual in Sufism," was not quite as successful: "Most interesting personal experience. Stylistically needs more refinement. 'B'." Some of the "accidental" initiations described in this section will identify Murshid Sam as a contemporary Mulla Nasruddin.

"Murshid's history looks as if it came out of something more bizarre than even "The Arabian Nights." For behind Sufism and the Sufi Orders there is that Hierarchy which controls the destinies of the world. Only this Hierarchy is not only manifesting through Islam, it manifests above and beyond all religions."

Diaries – Oct. 16, 1964

SUFI VISION
AND INITIATION

The great Al-Ghazzali has written, "TASSAWUF (Sufism) CONSISTS OF EXPERIENCES AND NOT PREMISES." One must support the contention of Titus Burckhardt also, that one can not really understand Sufism without going through the Sufi disciplines. This is a living testimonial of a Sufi who has passed the tests.

The mystic is one who has had the experience of Divinity-Infinity. Many people have experiences of Divinity without touching Infinity. Because of them we have the contemporary motto, "God is dead." But many also have touched Infinity without Divinity. There has been a whole school of this centering around Dr. Bucke and his self-selected "Cosmic Consciousness."

One who has reached the real Infinity finds himself at one with Life, especially with his fellow-creatures. . . . But a true mystic has often to face the ignominy of the whole society. Indeed there is a school among the Sufis called Malamatia, which means "blameworthy," who are expected to become unpopular. And there is one note common to all pseudo-mystics, that they seek popularity.

Once one has met a real Mystic, it becomes easy to distinguish the true from the false. The first vision I had of Pir-O-Murshid Hazrat Inayat Khan was in 1921. He appeared to me on five different levels and said: "Fear not, I shall always be with you." There followed a long period of pain and tribulation, but the consciousness of the Pir grew and grew until one entered the next state, called fana-fi-Rassoul (absorption into the Christ).

Just before Hazrat Inayat Khan's arrival in California in 1923, I saw him once again in Vision. In the Vision I was going toward the Southern Pacific Station to greet the Murshid. Being of nervous disposition, I began to run and I saw the train approaching with the head of the Murshid (Hazrat Inayat Khan) projecting from the smokestack. But I was too anxious, and my heart-body projected from my subtle body, and at the same time the Murshid's heart-body projected. The two heart-bodies rushed at each other like two comets and melted and molded, becoming One; and this One became the Spirit of the Universe.

In coming into his room for an interview the following day (Summer Solstice), however, there was no person, only a tremendous Light. But it was not just Light; it was a tremendous feeling of binding Love. . .

This first experience with Hazrat Inayat Khan stayed with me for Life and continued to encourage me and strengthen me in performing His Work.

DYING

In March 1925, my pain was so great that I thought death was at hand. I went into seclusion in the wilderness. At sunset of the third day two doves appeared and circled my head. As night approached and I performed my spiritual practices I felt the presence of Khwaja Khizr (the legendary Green Man of the desert), sometimes identified with Elijah, who was the spiritual teacher of Moses as described in Quran. He appeared three evenings in succession, finally offering me poetry, music, or longevity as a gift. I chose poetry, but the others have followed over the years.

In 1926 I called on Inayat Khan, and he verified the events of 1925 during the six interviews he granted me. One of these interviews was concerned with the science of commentary.

"Hazrat Inayat Khan asked your Murshid to write commentaries on his writings, and your Murshid could not. Then exactly three years after his death he manifested and began dictating these commentaries, according to the capacity of your Murshid. And neither the language nor the wisdom belong to your Murshid but are products of *fana-fi-sheikh* and *tassawuri Murshid*."

Diaries – Jan. 25, 1964

DANCE OF THE PROPHETS

After the Vision of Khwaja Khizr in 1925, FANA-FI-RASSOUL was experienced. In succession, all the great Prophets of all the world's religions appeared, and Sam was absorbed into each in turn. I performed a ritual and it ended by perceiving in broad daylight the procession of the Messengers of God who formed a circle to perform a Cosmic Dance, whereupon they all merged into One. I saw the Prophet Mohammed double and the others singly and took this as a sign to begin Quranic studies. I had already studied most other scriptures by that time. Finally, in Vision, the Prophet bestowed a robe, which was later actually received before the tomb of Moineddin Chisti in Ajmir, India.

"At the Dargah I was given a strange blessing in Vision, with two types of tassels put around me, and later a robe and shirt with the instructions that I was henceforth to represent Christian Sufism in all non-Islamic countries. This was confirmed by Syed Farook Hussain Chisti, my Hadim (Guide) before I could confirm it verbally."

Diaries, Oct. 22, 1956

THE ROBE

A similar confirmation occurred in 1962 when the author was given a robe in Vision, this time by the poet Amir Khusraw. Before I could report it, it was bestowed on me in physical form by my present Pir-O-Murshid, Sufi Barkat Ali of West Pakistan. The value of the robe (*khirka*) is specially mentioned by the poet Hafiz-i-Shirazi, and I can assure you that its very wearing produces a marked change in one's behavior pattern. This takes two forms, a 'sober' and a 'drunken' state. Any type of criticism, opposition or contempt throws one into the 'drunken' state (*sukr*), and vastly increases one's immediate *insight*. Therefore one loves one's "enemies" for a very strange reason. By oneself one cannot evoke that State. (*hal*).

"In Lahore I walked into a shop and started making purchases. The merchant hailed me and explained that I could not buy anything more as God had put a limit on my purchases. I told him my name was "Murad", meaning that I was under grace and therefore different from a "mureed" who was under the guidance of a spiritual teacher.

A man standing nearby overheard me and identified himself as a "mureed." As a result of that 'chance' meeting, I was taken to an assembly of Nakshibandis, witnessed their ceremonials, took part in their Zikar and was given a cap and beads.

The khalif in charge was very handsome,

with beautiful eyes showing love and spiritual light. After the experience of the meeting I told one of the mureeds that I had never seen a man more like Jesus Christ than their khalif. 'You should see our murshid,' came the reply."

Diaries – Nov. 18, 1956

Once one has contacted the Messengers of God, one will never confuse Them. They are at the same time both the incarnation or humanization of the Spirit of the Universe, yet different from each other. To the Arabs Jesus is known as Ruh-i-Allah or the 'Spirit of God.'

In Sufic terms Akhlak Allah means to act as if in the Presence of God. I differ from those who say only certain passages in Quran indicate Mysticism. The whole thing shows that the Prophet was in constant Awareness of God. So was Swami Ramakrishna just before our time.

FANA-FI-RASSOUL

I was living in semi-seclusion in the woods of South Carolina in 1946 when Hazrat Inayat Khan would appear every day. One day while brushing my teeth, a tooth fell out, the very one missing in the Prophet Mohammed's mouth. (I later learned that there is a school of Sufis in North Africa whose initiation consists in knocking out that same tooth.) Hazrat Inayat Khan appeared and laughed and laughed. The next day Rassoul Mohammed appeared.

During the following period both Jesus Christ and Mohammed appeared intermittently. I have seen Jesus in so many guises. He has never appeared to me looking like Galahad but in human form exactly as Kahlil Gibran pictured him; but seldom has He appeared in human form,but usually as the Spirit of the Universe.

IN THE NAME OF ALLAH

Sufis teach Allah as *Zat* (essence) and *Sifat* (qualities). The *Zat* equals *Nirguna Brahma* and the Hebraic *Ain Soph*. In the early stages (of training), disciples (*mureeds* or *talibs*) repeat *Wazifas*, phrases emphasizing the qualities of God. It is only in *tassawuri Mohammed* that all these qualities are combined, synthesized, and conjoined. When one walks *in* or *with* Mohammed's footsteps, he comes to the perfection of the qualities in action. Thus Mohammed has been pictured as the PERFECT MAN by Al-Jili.

"The Muslims constantly say "Allaho Akbar" (God is Great). I could write books on this one phrase alone. . . . In life I use it and the first step is to repeat the phrase. Because it is in Arabic and as first used in this form by Mohammed, most people will not try it. I have used it and it changed me from a timid

215

introvert to an exuberant extrovert. This is just one phrase."

Diaries — March 26, 1964

Although FANA-FI-LILLAH means "effacement in the Universal Spirit," we must remember that always "in God we live and move and have our being." Inayat Khan taught that the Murshid acts as a Cupid to bring the Soul to God, and that: "God is our only teacher. We all learn from Him."

I RECEIVE MY NAME

Ten years after I had received the name of A. Murad in Vision, by the Prophet, I found myself stranded in Dacca, Pakistan. Through a strange set of circumstances I was taken to a courtyard where there was a group of Sufis. One of them, named Wahab, demanded:

"Who is your Murshid?"

"Sufi Inayat Khan."

"Pir-O-Murshid Sufi Inayat Khan?", he asked with surprise. "Why, it is his writings I am translating into Bengali."

Then he introduced me to (Sheikh) Maulana Ghafour (Chisti), who initiated me into the Chistia Order and gave me the name Ahmed Murad.

When I came to the tomb of Moineddin Chisti, Founder of the Order using his name and which uses music (and dance) for spiritual development, there was a huge crowd gathered. My guide instructed,

216

"Close your eyes. What do you see?"

Closing my eyes, I felt the presence of a man who gave me a robe (it has always been the same robe), but this Vision was different from any before because it was the same with eyes open and closed. I tried opening and closing my eyes many times. Always the same.

Then my guide asked me my name.

"Ahmed Murad."

He said, "From now on, it is Ahmed Murad Chisti."

That evening there was a musical performance. Everyone sat in a square, one side with Hindus, on the other side women without veils, and Sufi disciples on the other two sides. I have never heard such uplifting music. There is nothing like it in the whole West. There is some 'uplift' from Eastern rites and also from the Sufi ceremonies in the Near East, but they did not have the tremendous effect on the heart and consciousness. It is like being bathed in an infinite ocean of love. . . .

"One day we were studying Masnavi when Pir-O-Murshid (Hazrat) appeared and told me, 'Be a Flute.'
I became a flute and this flute is heard in two ways — as the Flute-of-Krishna and as the Flute-of-Rumi. . . and I carry this inner music and it may be given to the world, Inshallah ['God-willing']".

Diaries – March 27, 1963

IN NORTH AFRICA

My experiences with the Sufis in North Africa were no less significant than the experiences in India and Pakistan, but here they will be described in brief. When I arrived in Cairo, the Grand (Rifai) Sheikh appeared to me in Vision and gave me detailed instructions. The next day I heard of a grand convocation at the tomb of Sidi Shirani in celebration of his birthday. I decided to attend, although I did not know what would happen if I came uninvited.

As soon as I took off my shoes and crossed the threshold, two arms grabbed me.

"Well," I thought, "the Lewises have tread where fools fail to go one time too many; they've finally got you."

The next thing I knew I was escorted to a microphone and found that I was guest speaker of the evening. One does not know how these things occur.

After the formalities, the ritual began. We stood variously in a circle, a square, and a Maltese cross. There was singing with symphonies and antiphonies exactly as I had read about early Church music. The modes were distinctly European, not like the Arabic or Near Eastern types and decidedly tonic and harmonic. It was a very long affair and I did everything right, following what the Sheikh had instructed in Vision the night before.

"When I arrived at Luxor I was met at the hotel by a registering clerk who would accept no tip. When he saw my tasbih (prayer beads), he exclaimed:
"I want that."
"Nothing doing," I replied, as it was my special treasure. When he kept insisting, I explained that I could not let him have the beads because not only was I already a teacher and was using them, but also because I could only give them to a Sheikh.
"I am the Sheikh," the clerk said.
He was too. Naturally I gave him the tasbih."

Diaries — Sept 2, 1960

On the 17th day of September, which was Sunday, was I commanded to write when the Spirit of the Lord appeared unto me.

When the message of Sufism was presented to the Western World it was clothed in the ideal of love & harmony & beauty. how it might have been clothed in other ideals but it was clothed in these ideals; the ideal of love the ideal of harmony & the ideal of beauty. But it is one thing to talk of ideals & it is another thing to practise them. It is still another thing to practise these ideals within the domain of the traditions of Sufism & the Grace of God.

We cannot by command control the Divine Grace nor can we obtain it through the offense hearts. Many times in the past has the message of Sufism been inhibited by the hindrances placed before mureeds hindrances not in the

DATES FROM THE

DIARIES

Sam was often seen chuckling to himself. His diaries and letters show why. They also reveal a bold personality with a clear Vision of this New Age and a soul deeply immersed in God.

He told one disciple: "I'm concerned with famine and flood relief in the Orient and comic relief in the Occident."

OATES:

DIARY SELECTIONS

THE GREAT FLOOD

I heard this story from a sixty-seven year old housewife in Guy Mills, Pennsylvania.

There was an old farmer in this district who had lived through the Johnstown Flood and was always anxious to tell everybody about it. He would not only insist on talking to the young, but grabbed every tourist, and it was always the same theme.

He finally passed on in his nineties, to the relief of the citizens who had become bored.

The story is that he went to heaven and St. Peter asked him if there was anything he wanted. "Yes, I should like to tell the folks about the Johnstown Flood." "Wish granted."

So St. Peter whispered to him: "Remember, you may say anything you want, but please bear in mind, Noah is in the audience."

January 2, 1963

TWO, ONE, OR ZERO?

I asked Nyogen Senzaki: "When Sogen Asahina and Sam Lewis met, were there two, one or no people in the room?"

"Let us have some tea," was his reply. I knew then that Nyogen Senzaki would soon leave the earth.

May 11, 1968

ORGANIC GARDEN

The book of bitterness is closed. A new cycle has definitely begun. It is obvious that there is a huge integrative movement going on. This may be indicative of the Aquarian Age, for something like this is certainly happening. The group has displaced the individual, but it is a dynamic, organic group, demonstrating "I am the Vine and ye are the branches thereof."

December 1, 1968

The hardest hazard has not been evil but the obstacle of facing disciples of "great" teachers, that each and all tend to worship the teacher and not live according to the principles he announced.

April 15, 1965

'TIS A GIFT TO BE SIMPLE

Samuel asked God when the Kingdom of Heaven would come, and he got this answer:
When the weaver is permitted to discourse on Kabir,
And the cook explains the teachings of Shankaracharya,
When the carpenter occupies the Christian pulpit,
And the camel driver displaces the mullah in the mosque
And professor and pundit nevermore use the word *humility*.

May 2, 1965

"So many go around claiming God-Experience, and when they ask Sam, he always says: 'Never mind their claims. Show me their disciples.'"

February 12, 1969

A LITTLE CHILD SHALL LEAD THEM

The Bible says that "the lamb and the lion shall lie down together, and a little child shall lead them." But the little children know better. They know what the metaphysicians and preachers never can fathom. So I have given my secrets to the little children.

May 2, 1965

Actually, Buddhism, poetry and mythology have become luxuries, for all one's efforts are toward the solution of food problems.

May 2, 1965

BIOLOGICAL BROTHERHOOD

The "spiritual brotherhood" is an operation in which persons act as if part of an organic whole; the principle is the same that we can see in biological transformations, that individuals, operating as cells, produce as if in a more complex (I shun the word "higher" here) living organism or entity which goes ahead and seems to carry them along — drops of water in a river or cells in a volvox. . .

August 28, 1965

225

GOD IN EVERYTHING

The Ramakrishna Mission is tops in India . . . . In my discussions last night I said you can measure a spiritual person by the enlightenment of those in his presence, and this was agreed. The Ramakrishna people and the Sufis transmit light, but the Ramakrishna people withdraw at least from meat and marriage, and the Sufis see God in everything.

October 14, 1958

PEACE

It is the inner peace which is real. Words are not peace. Thoughts are not peace. Plans are not peace. Programs are not peace. Peace is fundamental, but it is hard to appreciate, hard to experience and hard to realize. It is fundamental to all faiths, all religions, all spirituality.

The difference between Logos-Peace and our "peace" is that our peace is a vacuum, a zero, a nothing, a blank, a negative to the extreme; the Logos-Peace is fullness, is all-inclusive, is brotherhood. The human body is a society of myriads of personalities which must work together in and with and under God. This must be experiences and not syllogical, truth and not truism. Every Transcendentalist poet of America knew it and every newsman today seems to work against it. We must have *excitement*; excitement is the death of peace.

March 22, 1965

WILL THE REAL SHEIKH . . .

When I arrived in Port Said I hailed a taxi cab because something about the driver attracted me. We began discussing Sufism quite spontaneously. The driver mentioned he was a member of the Rifai Order. I mentioned that I had just recently been initiated into the Rifais (who are known in the West as the "howling dervishes").

"Who is your sheikh?" I asked politely. "I would like to meet him."

The driver turned around: "I am the sheikh."

September 2, 1960

The Sufis have a saying: "Say ALLAH and leave them to their devices."

May 18, 1964

THUNDERBOLT DANCE

Nyogen Senzaki appeared, took over my being, threw thunderbolts and caused confusion. Actually this is the work of Fudo Bosatsu [the Protector of the Dharma, whom Sam identified with] and it is no fun. You have to smash everybody, friend or foe, to get rid of illusion. There is a vast difference between the thunderbolt and some of the "nice" dance patterns I have seen based on it.

August 11, 1963

227

Richard Alpert has been around here. He has been lecturing as Baba Ram Dass and acts as if he were a character from *A Catcher in the Rye*. He has been very successful in drawing huge crowds of the young, not mentioned by the press of course.

February 2, 1970

Those who have seen my diaries think I am very conceited and self-centered. I write what happens. Master Tun Loo has written what happens. He is like a child; he does not know all the humbug and bugaboos of metaphysicians and professors . . . . But when you come to Master Tun Loo you not only learn what he is, but if you listen closely you find out also what you are . . . .

September 23, 1963

Ever since I was a child I have been moved by the biblical passage: "My house shall be a house of prayer for all peoples." It seemed to me at an early age that some Jewish people were destined to return to Palestine. But the history of "Lawrence of Arabia," the blind following of Baal Peor (Balfour) instead of Moses, the repudiation of tradition for political zealousness shows that we are still in a world which confuses words with things, and clinging to words has replaced the attainment of an ideal.

October 21, 1963

WHEN THE GODS ARRIVE . . .

The New Age is here; I meet the people more and more and more, but they will not be led by the phonies of another age. When the gods arrive, the half-gods go.

November 12, 1965

When I first studied Buddhism — and it seems to have been largely forgotten — we used to end our letters:
May all people be peaceful!
May all people be blissful!
May all people be happy!

May 9, 1964

I am teaching Sufism as Science, not as a religion in any old sense, but as a Science cum Devotion. We work with the Names of God . . .

August 1, 1967

SUFISM MEANS

Sufism used to mean "Divine Wisdom" and so far as Sam is concerned it still does. It still means that the Divine Voice constantly comes from within. It still means "speaking the word that is put into the mouth." It still means growth in the states and stages of consciousness into ever-growing Divine Awareness; and it still means "one single Brotherhood in the Fatherhood of God."

December 1, 1967

DO UNTO OTHERS . . .

The Sufi not only prays to God, he represents God. By this I mean that he not only asks for Love and Wisdom and Joy and Peace, he does everything possible to awaken Love and Light and Wisdom and Joy and Peace in others.

December 1, 1967

MURSHID AND MUREED

The new age is different because all the young people see if one is practicing or verbalizing. You cannot fool them. And in turn one practices "Murshid and mureed are one." This is not symbology but actuality.

January 17, 1968

In Sufism we call Allah the All-Sufficient and depend on nobody. Love is not dependent, it is mutual. Joy is not dependent, it is mutual. Peace is not dependent. It is.

June 12, 1968

DANCE

Sam had already begun the Astrological dancing when Vilayat Khan spoke on the Cosmic Dances of the Sufis and their relation to the ancient Pythagorean school. So the next lesson was when Sam began putting into practice one by one what Vilayat had spoken about.

July 3, 1968

Finding so many young people ready, this person began to teach openly what might be called "Occult Dancing." It is not a very good word. This person did not wish to do this teaching, but there is no one else who is prepared to. The first phases are "The Dances of the Stars"; the second, "The Dances of the Elements"; the third, "Cosmic Dancing." The first two were derived from Hazrat Inayat Khan and the latter from Ruth St. Denis. But the time has come, the receptacles are ready, and this is the new age . . . .

THE EXCEPTION WHICH PROVES . . .

Dervish Dancing has been started by this person and one hopes in time that people will say, as Ghaus-i-Azam said to Moineddin Chisti: "For you, music is permitted." [Koran forbids music and dance as entertainment.]

August 2, 1963

It is easy to demonstrate that there is great joy in the contact of human bodies; this pales into insignificance before the contact of the subtle bodies. This is being demonstrated in the Dervish dances. In turn this is paled when there is the living contact between the hearts which is demonstrated in Darshan and in one form of the Krishna dances . . .

The Sufis teach: The lover is a vain thing, the beloved is all in all.

October, 1968

Ram Dass means "servant of God." This is what Mohammed called himself — Abdullah, which means Ram Dass, exactly the same. Mohammed said: "I am the servant of God. Call me nothing but Messenger and servant of God."

July 23, 1963

THIS IS THE TEMPLE OF GOD

There is a great resonance which takes place in singing the Ram Nam using the head as a dome. Now the resonance has become complete, using and vibrating the whole body, demonstrating what is taught but not studied in the Christian Bible: "The human body is the temple of the Holy Spirit."

December 24, 1969

SONG AND DANCE

Outwardly Sam's work is through "Dances of Universal Peace." Along with that has been the choral group singing hymns and themes drawn from the real religions of the past, but integrating according to the contemporary types of music, which are becoming universal and international. [This is a reference to the Sufi Choir, which has recorded three records since Murshid's passing.]

The Divine Spirit does not manifest as any thought-form; still less as an orthodoxy. We have done it, or it has been done through us, by Ram.

December 21, 1970

It is time for man to exhibit those attributes which he ascribes to a Deity. I am teaching the Divine Epithets now through the Dance. I had hoped to do it through sound and voice and this is still possible, but it is being done through the Dance, and one does not care anymore whether one is accepted or not. The rise in mystical consciousness of those who participate is sufficient evidence.

January 27, 1969

I HAVE COME TO DESTROY RELIGION AND BRING GOD

As one sage has said, "I have come to destroy religion and bring God." Actually he only brought his ego, but there is no question that religion is disintegrating and all the more because it is a legend that religion has anything to do with morality. The purpose of religion is to get people to come to a particular church with a particular belief and particular ritual. I teach that Allah is closer than the neck vein and try to make people aware of it, actually.

February 16, 1969

Sam has as his koan, so to speak, the first words of Handel's *Messiah:* "Every valley shall be exalted and every hill laid low; the crooked places made straight."

March 11, 1970

233

THE STONE THAT IS REJECTED . . .

No doubt there is a time for all things. And now instead of lapsing into the presumable securities of old age, Sam's life is becoming more and more public. No doubt it requires considerable patience when one's theme, so to speak, is "The stone that is rejected is become the cornerstone."

March 11, 1970

DANCE WITHOUT DEVOTION

Tonight we shall give the last rehearsals of one of Sam's ras-lila (play of Krishna) dances. The technique is simple. The steps are easy. But without extreme devotion it is utterly impossible to perform.

March 11, 1970

SHOW ME THEIR DISCIPLES

So many go around claiming God-experience and when they ask Sam, he always says: "Never mind their claims. Show me their disciples." And we hear stories of the rise and fall of this great personality and that, but never a sign of any great disciple. So many churches and so many cults, but only the young experience God, so we shall have a New Age in which the God-people may be separate, in a certain sense, from the Church people.

February 12, 1969

MONUMENTS

A salaam aleikum. We may keep a phrase as a motto or we may weave it into our lives. Religion has failed because sacred words have been turned into mottos . . ."

February 16, 1969

ALI VERSUS MOHAMMED

The Shias asked whether Sufi Ahmed Murad [S.A.M.] thought Ali was as great or greater than Mohammed. He said, "Ali was always aware of Allah. Mohammed was aware of Allah and also of mankind as well. Thus he was the Perfect Man." They accepted this explanation.

February 6, 1969

Our efforts to bring Arabs and Israelies together threaten to snowball. We have Jews saying Allah and Muslims repeating the Shemah. You would imagine some editor might be interested. Ha. Ha.

August 2, 1970

OM SRI RAM JAI RAM JAI JAI RAM!

It seems that the time has come when the human soul is finding more joy in chanting Holy phrases and in praising God, than in anything else.

September 4, 1970

AT LAMA

Then we came to Lama which may well become the center of a sort of American Lama-ism. While I am here to present Sufism it became obvious that something more is in the wind. Both Sufism and Mahayana teach the transcendental intuition (kashf or prajna, and no nonsense). It is operational and it has made me bang down hard on rump-ritualism called "Zen", which ignores the fact that Zen is prajna (insight or wisdom) and not dhyana (meditation).

The Quran teaches that the Divine Light is neither of the East nor West, and I presented that therefore the Rockies were as Holy as the Himalayas, and that this was the place to present the Maha Mudra Meditation . . .

Faithfully,
Rev. He Kwang [S.A.M.]
June 2, 1970

JUST HUMAN BEINGS

So here I am in a spiritual commune way up in the Rockies [Lama], where they practice, practice, practice what others preach, preach, preach. It is marvelous. It is the New Age. It is the New Age without any recent Messiahs. Just human beings who demonstrate love and humanity, and worship according to the forms of all religions and don't waste time on endless lectures.

June 6, 1970

GINSBERG'S REVOLUTION

When the well-known Allen Ginsberg was in this region hardly a handful supported the idea of a social revolution, while thousands of people — nearly all young — repeated mantrams in joy and welcomed a spiritual revolution.

Om Sri Ram, Jai Ram, Jai Jai Ram!

June 3, 1970

SUFIZEN

And now the determination to do for Sufism what Philip Kapleau (in *The Three Pillars of Zen*) has done for Zen. Indeed I visited the Zendo of Roshi Taisan in New York and was amazed with the types there, all seemingly young people who have had satori or even moksha. So one is very careful not to insist that his way is "the only way."

November 27, 1970

NO TIME

Last night I had the largest group of young Americans chanting "La Illaha El Illahu;" "Mohammedah Rasul-Lillah." I have had no time for Orthodoxy; I have had nothing but time for Kalama and Zikar [chanting the phrases].

December 10, 1970

A General Semanticist may be a verbalist; sometimes he must be; a Meta-Semanticist may also use words, but he must connect them in the same manner as a statistician uses graphs.

For example, I throw at you certain problems and words which General Semantics has bypassed:

ECOLOGY   POLLUTION   MIDDLE CLASS
DRUG   PSYCHIC   PSYCHEDELIC
HALLUCINATION   ENVIRONMENT
PHOSPHATE   DETERIORATION
PROGRESSION   EVOLUTION   EDUCATION

June 10, 1970

It may be that through the aid of the Message the people of Palestine will become more peaceful and reconciled to each other, and the peoples of India more warlike and willing to struggle for justice. The Hindus can not rightfully neglect their Scriptures, in one of which (The Bhagavad Gita) Avatar Krishna has said, 'Therefore fight, O Arjuna;' and the Hebrews will have to learn to beat their mental swords into pruning hooks; and by such means the will of the Semite and the karma of Hindu will become assimilated in the holy teachings and practice of the Message.

December 23, 1969

My main theme has always been that of Imam Al-Ghazzali, that Sufism is based on experiences and not premises.

November 27, 1970

Last night some words were read from my epic poem, "Saladin", about Ram-Sita. In the pursuit of fana-fi-Rassoul [effacement in the prophet] when this person was under the direct guidance of Mecca Shereef, he was shown the eminence of all the so-called 'Avatars' of India and made to accept them from and on their level and not from his tradition, personal views or the opinions of the community. The poem read was the stanza about Ram-Sita and the audience was of Yogi-chelas to whom this person never speaks of Tassawuf [Sufism]. And they were very much moved, but at no time could he tell them: "My Sadguru is Mohammad Mecca Shereef, Khatimal-i-Nabun", for they are not ready and would be unsettled. Likewise the so-called 'Muslims' have their private *affirmation* which they call 'Islam', each his own and thus the world is divided.

March 3, 1965

TO MANIFEST CHRIST

To manifest Christ it is necessary to manifest love and tenderness and strength. From another point of view, the amalgamation of love, tenderness and strength means the Christ-consciousness.

November 11, 1969

ALLAH WHO?

My first efforts after 1945 were to encourage meetings between the spiritual leaders of Israel and Islam. Representatives from both groups accepted the offer but questioned whether the other "camp" had real spiritual persons in it . . . . This plan will be realized some day.

October 21, 1963

The dances of Universal Peace have gotten out of hand, as they should. I feel I am a conveyor and instrument rather than author.

December 22, 1969

FOUR-DIMENSIONAL TEACHING

We have gone through the phases of simple art and concentration practices . . . But a higher dimension has intervened in the form of Dance, ritual, and pageant. One could hardly imagine the effects of three and four dimensional application of the Gatha studies [the esoteric papers of Hazrat Inayat Khan]. This is what is being taken up today.

This will mean the reproduction of the eternal Mysteries to the human race. These dances first come in visions at night with no explanations. It generally takes three nights before they are clear mentally. The Vision comes with no explanations. It proves later to be totally rational.

November 11, 1969

"There is no compulsion in Islam" and, we may add,
"There is no compulsion in tassawuf [Sufism]."

November 9, 1969

MOINEDDIN CHISTI

Our work here with dancing is entirely in line
with the work of Moineddin Chisti himself.
[Moineddin Chisti brought Sufism to India and
combined Indian ragas and Persian poetry.] It is
more than possible that we shall be performing
historically a mission in the Western world
comparable to his of an earlier period.

September 15, 1969

The World is awakening.

December 1970

THE LAST TEMPTATION OF KRISHNA

Sri Krishna is the most difficult [attunement] for
Sam. It makes him fall in love with all the women
and they with him. And Sam has around him some of
the most beautiful young women he has ever seen.
When he began the Krishna dances he was
ashamed, but Allah/Ram said to him: "For others it
may be wrong, but for you it is not wrong because
there is no lust." Then Sam realized that Sri Krishna
could appear and dance with men Gopis.

August 18, 1968

241

Being stupid or enlightened enough to find God in all mountains, and more especially, the mountains whence Jesus Christ delivered the Beatitudes and celebrated, I find that wisdom emanates from many mountains and from many people dwelling on those many mountains in all parts of the world. This of course is heresy to all the "world saviours" "avatars", etc. etc.

December 22, 1969

GOD IS THE ONLY TEACHER

The essential of all knowledge, wisdom and morality is God (whom I prefer to call either Allah or Ram). Inayat Khan said, "God is the only Teacher, we all learn from Him."

July 3, 1968

BOOK OF
COSMIC PROPHECY

The great Zen teacher, Sokei-An Sasaki, showed this person ways of having the cosmic picture, with a warning that both the picture and the person seeing it would be filled with terror. The whole history of the world from 1931 to 1946 was unfolded.

(Commentary on Mental Purification)

The Book of Cosmic Prophecy sheds light on the tragic events of the 1930's and '40's and shows how God works through global affairs. Written from 1932 to 1946 in the voice of the Prophet Samuel, the powerful poetic rhetoric and sense of authority is strikingly Old Testament in flavor. Hazrat Inayat Khan said of the mission of the prophet:

"The prophets were sent to awaken man; just as someone who cannot wake up of his own accord in the morning is wakened by the alarm clock."

("The Prophetic Tendency,"
The Sufi Message, Vol. VIII, p. 34)

Selections From

COSMIC PROPHECY

Toward the One, the Perfection of Love, Harmony and Beauty, the Only Being, united with All the Illuminated Souls who form the Embodiment of the Master, the Spirit of Guidance.

"ARISE AND PROPHESY"

January 31, 1932

And the Lord said, "Arise and prophesy unto the children of men as did your forefathers.
Arise and convey to them My Will and My decrees
For as it has been in the days of yore, so shall it be again"
And He said unto me, "Samuel, what tasteth thou?"
I answered, "O Lord, the taste of blood is in my mouth
And the taste of blood is in my heart
And the taste of blood is in my inner being."
He answered, "Thou speakest truly, for the taste of blood is the taste of war.
As it is in you, so it is in the world and will surely follow."
Then the taste of blood continued in my mouth and in my heart and in my inner being.

For three days did the taste of blood remain, neither at day nor at night did it depart.

And at the end of three days in the evening did the voice of the Lord appear.

And when the Voice of the Lord appeared the taste of blood disappeared.

Then said Beth Kol,

"Behold that the taste of blood was the blood of men

Verily this day on earth has the city of Shanghai been taken

And innocent babes slaughtered at their mother's breasts.

Innocent men and women and children killed and maimed and robbed.

Therefore arise and turn thy face against the men of Yamato

Against the men of Yamato and the women of Yamato and the children of Yamato, the fire of the Lord is kindled.

What they this day have done upon earth so it is being done to them in Heaven.

Their islands shall tremble, their islands shall sink

Earthquakes and famine and pestilence shall destroy the land.

The walls of Yokohama are falling, the shipping is again destroyed

The selfishness and greed of rulers is repaid

I knocked and they would not listen.

I called and they would not heed. . . ."

"CHINA BATHED IN BLOOD"

February 5, 1932

Bandits!
With the wailing of a thousand bleeding infants.
Dying mothers with babes in arms
And the shattered ruins of a mighty city
Walls fallen on helpless men and women,
Crushed amid the smoldering debris
And the pitter patter of a rain of bullets.
Bandits!
Where the craven lusty men in uniform
Charge with bayonets upon little students
Raking with shellfire the homes of peaceful people,
Crying 'This must be for the sake of order and
    peace'.
Force apologizes to force in the name of Civilization
And taunts the weak as pariahs of the earth.
Thus Buddha is avenged as Christ before Him.
And China bathed in blood.
Bandits!
Aye! The Perfect One is now become the scapegoat
Whose missionaries serve the hand of mammon,
And murder lurks beneath the yellow robe.
The wisteria is bathed with scarlet hue
And the cherry blossom a symbol of tyranny.

Is this the best that man can do to man?
To hurl a holocaust upon the timid
And smash the innocent in Moloch's arms?

Then doomed is civilization
And the bystander and warrior down together
Shall go when Justice flees away from the earth.

May this not be;
May some mightier power arise
To sink these murderers in ignominy
And save the world from falling in the dust
CHINA Your night will pass
The dawn will rise and see you once more free.
Leader in all the humane arts as of yore,
Proving to humanity who are the righteous
And leaving them freest choice to judge
Who are the bandits.

"PROPHESY
UNTO THE MEN OF YAMATO (JAPAN)"

February 9, 1932

Thus sayeth the Lord thus speaketh the Holy One,
Girdle your loins and prophesy unto the men of
Yamato
Turn your face to the west, be unafraid.
Behold, the mountains shall erupt and the waves
beat violently
Torrent and cyclone and fury shall avenge Me
The rocks shall not keep still, nor the volcanoes
slumber
For this people has become a nation of criminals.

Of yore, there was a foundling, a bastard foundling,
And a kindly woman discovered him and suckled it
in her arms
Bathed it and clothed it and fed it with the fat of the
land.
Now has the foundling grown to adulthood and
turned his hand against his foster mother.
Her who gave him shelter he doth beat
And her who raised him from the dust he doth cast
to the dust.
Thus hath he sown terrible Karma and terrible
Karma shall he reap.
Having known the teachings of Sakya Muni and
Kung-tse
A thousand times more to blame .
The hour is coming the day draws near
When the blood of Yamato shall be shed in the
streets of Yamato.
When the houses of Nippon shall be in ruin
Rich and poor, high and low, Mikado and
riksha-bearer
Woe! Wail ye in Yokahama and Kobe
And shed your tears in Hakodate.
Ruin and famine spread in the land and the
earthquake shall again take its toll
The mountains shall erupt and the waves beat
violently
Torrent and cyclone and fury shall avenge her
And the glory of lust shall be sunk into the ground.

THE ETERNAL DHARMA

(On the closing of the Zen School in San Francisco)

May 6, 1932

Thus have I heard
The Blessed One the Holy-Enlightened One, the
    Supreme opened his eyes.
He breathed into a whisper
And there were rumblings of thunder and a mighty
    roar
Which were drowned in a gentle voice, a sublime
    voice, a most musical voice.
"The teachings of Tathagata are eternal.
The most noble teachings of the Tathagata are not
    to be compared with other teachings.
The teachings of Tathagata are for all men.
When the most noble Dharma was rejected in
    Bharata, was it preached in Kitai? or Chin?
When the Sangha in Kitai and Chin no longer
    preserved the noble truths was the chain of
    Bodhisattvas and Arhats continued in Hondu
    (Japan)?
Now that the people of Nippon have rejected the
    most noble teachings,
Now that they have ceased to live according to the
    eightfold path,
Now that they seek in waste places for vain
    treasures,
So shall the light of all the Buddhas be withdrawn
    from them

As it was withdrawn from Bharata and Kitai so shall
    it be withdrawn from them
And as empires of Sind and of the Yellow Land fell
    when the spiritual law was forsaken,
So shall the land of Nippon and the people of Nippon
    suffer.
But the teaching of the Tathagata is eternal.
The most noble four-truths
And the most noble doctrine of Arya Dharma, the
    eightfold path,
These shall continue and continue
And if the Middle Kingdom shall accept them again
The teachings will be accepted and the people
    blessed
And if the Aryavartans accept them
The teachings will be accepted and the people
    blessed.
But if the people of the Yellow Empire reject them
    as the men of Nippon reject them,
If the scions of Aryavarta incorporate them not into
    their law,
Then shall the most noble teachings of the
    Tathagata not perish.
The teachings will not perish, cannot perish
But then shall these teachings be incorporated with
    other teachings.
The truths about the Buddha and the Dharma and
    the Sangha,
The four most noble truths and the eight-fold path of
    deliverance
These shall not disappear but shall be incorporated
    with the teachings of the other Enlightened Ones

So that the teachings of all the Buddhas shall be one.
The doctrines of all the Bodhisattvas shall be united
And the glory even from Gautama unto Maitreya
    shall be one glory
And the light of the universe be poured upon all
    men."

"THE DOOM OF GERMANY"

May 9, 1932

The doom of the Ashkenazi (Germans)
Say: Ye shall not be doomed
But insofar as you turn against the children of the
    Lord
Then shall ye be doomed.
Insofar as ye turn unto your self-will
Then shall ye continue to suffer.
Yours was a fair country, a glorious country, a
    country of promise
Yours was becoming the elected among the nations.
Then in the wars ye failed to give a just peace
To the people of Hruska (Russia) and the people of
    Roum (Turkey)
Ye failed to give a just peace.
Now for fifteen years ye suffer as ye have sown.
The thorn and the briar intended for others has
    become your food.
The lash and the whip prepared for others has been
    hurled against your backs.

The servitude of others has been redeemed against
yourselves.
Now before you is the pardon of your Lord or the
worst of grievances.
Now before you is relief from trepidation
Or a thousandfold punishment.
Thus sayeth the Lord, the Holy One.
On that hour when you hurl the lash against my
people
Yours will be the fate of Sepharad and Lusitania and
Surmatia
Down shall ye go into barbarism.
Hand will be turned against hand, even brother
against brother.
The forest shall conquer the city and the tares the
pleasant fields
Woe, woe unto you who threaten danger
For upon you and all your people shall fall the doom.

"AMERICA"

May 10, 1932

Thus sayeth the Lord:

Now speak unto the people of thy land, which is a fair land and a promised land

A land of hope and a land of possibility.

O people of America, thus sayeth the Lord, the Holy One, the Keeper of the Covenants with humanity:

This nation was founded on the principles of justice and righteousness

This country was established to be a sanctuary for spiritual liberty.

Now that the people have gone after false gods,

Let them be admonished, let them be harangued, let them hear the word of the Lord.

For the covenant of America is with the Lord and not with Europe.

The covenant of America is with the Lord and not with Asia.

Foolish ones would establish agreements with the lands of Frankistan (France) of whom the nations are mad, wicked and deceitful

Other foolish ones seek pacts with Russia

The religion of their forefathers they desert for no religion

Else they seek a new religion.

Thus sayeth the Lord: Seek not a new religion but broaden your understanding.

Seek not a new faith but learn the meaning of faith.

Turn not to the materialism of Europe nor the magic of Asia.

But seek the Lord where He may be found.

The teachings for America were not inscribed in the hearts of prophets

Yet the words of Jefferson were true words, the words of Emerson were true words, the words of Whitman were true words.

Now though steeped in materialism ye shall arise

Though flooded by selfishness ye shall be rescued

Though near to drowning in inequity ye shall be saved.

On the morrow the teachings shall be spread through the land

The teachings of the West and the wisdom of the East

Christ and Buddha and Mohammed and Moses shall reign supreme

They and the sages of ancient and recent times

And a melting pot of the spirit shall there be therein

And all shall worship the Lord in rejoicing.

"TO THE ISLES OF ALBION (BRITAIN)"

10:30 May 10

Preach to the isles of the North Sea,
To the isles of Albion and Scotia saying
The word of the Lord hath come, the Word of the
    Lord hath come,
When the word of the Lord is here,
When the Shekinah of the Holy One approaches,
The wicked are afraid, the wicked shall be
    confounded.
Is God a God of this race or of that people?
Is God the possession of a kingdom or a
    government?
Say: Religion is the service of God.
Revealed in righteousness and well being to one's
    brethren
Blessed are they who control their subjects in peace
But woe unto them who oppress and abase
Who oppress their people at home and abase them
    that are afar.
The government shall fail, the wicked shall utterly
    perish.
But from the soil of Albion shall arise a new hope, a
    new glory
They who essayed to conquer the world through
    mastery shall achieve glory through surrender.
The empire over dominion shall be no more
But the empire of the spirit shall be borne
Whose navies shall be removed from the sea

But whose knowledge shall sweep over all lands.
Instead of father and tyrant to the men of dark skin
Brethren to all men.

O Albion! let thy glories be of the heart and mind
And the wickedness of the hand be withdrawn
forever.

"THE LAND OF PALESTINE"

May 12, 1932

Then the Lord spoke saying,
"Open thine eyes, Samuel and relate what thou dost
see."
I said, "O Lord, I see a vast desert, a barren desert
of sand."
The Lord said,"Thou seest truly for this is the land
of Palestine
And its barrenness is due to the barrenness in the
hearts of men
And the barrenness of Israel and also to the
barrenness of the Nazarenes and Muslims."
And he said, "Look thou again."
So I looked and I saw nought but a falling rain, no
land nor sea, nor sky, only falling floods of water.
Then God spoke declaring,
"This rain is my Mercy which never doth cease,
But when the hearts of men are hardened like a rain
which stops in midair

It touches not the ground; there is no room for it."
Then He said: "Look thou once more."
And behold I saw a single sprig above the ground,
A single shoot on the bare desert.
Then spake the Lord:
"Blessed be thou, O Israel, the redeemer of
humanity for now humanity is saved
The seeds of righteousness have remained beneath
the ground,
From generation unto generation they have
remained
From Baal Shem Tov unto this day hath there been
no prophet in Israel.
The sprig which thou seest is the fruit of Baal Shem
Tov,
That even the life of the Chassidim is not fully dead.
The life from the Gaonim and the Kabbalists has
been transmitted to this day.
Long have the seeds remained under the ground
And as to the Prophet Elijah, the sight of a small
cloud meant a drenching downpour,
So his single twig in essence contains hosts of
forests and fields.
For the children of Israel return to the land of their
fathers.
In matter they return to sow the vine and the corn
in Aretz (land) Yisroal
And in spirit they return to partake of the manna of
Heaven.
This day declare a new age and a new doctrine.
O men of Israel, no longer shall ye be a law unto
yourselves.

For the synagogue shall be open to all men or the synagogue shall go.
The cheder (school) shall not be for the Jehudim to the exclusion of the Goyim
And Talmud Torah shall be nought but the school of Holiness.
As the scriptures teach
'My temple shall be a house of prayer for all people'
So only shall that place be sanctified whose doors are open to all
The saint and sinner, the believer and the heretic, the men of old faiths and new faiths
All shall congregate in the synagogue of righteousness, in the temple of peace."

"THE WANDERING JEW"

(By the Sublime Master Jesus:)

June 30, 1932

Unto humanity I deliver my call and my cry,
For few have heard in the times that are past
And fewer still hear today,
I am the wandering Jew, one whom his people have
    forsaken,
But who has not forsaken his people.
Whosoever persecutes the children of Israel,
By me is he condemned to Hell.
You who wonder about Hitler, have patience, the
    Lord is patient.
Can you not see the cruelty in his eyes?
That shalt be burnt out and his followers doomed
I am the wandering Jew whom my people have not
    understood
And whom others have not been able to understand.
Is it my condemnation that they make me a god?
Who worshipped in the synagogue?
Who endeavored to restore the mystery of the
    Torah to my people?
Who served only God?
Now that my Father's will be done, all religions
    must recognize each one the others.
Until this is done will war on earth continue
And men be led astray.

"THE FUTURE OF THE UNITED STATES"

Nov. 9, 1932

Beloved Ones of God:

It is very interesting to consider the future of the United States as your country has been blessed by Allah. Actually an election is not nearly so important as some may imagine. As the human will is already known in heaven it can be perceived at any time by the keen mind. All an election does is to make the human will known to other wills.

There has grown up in America a false philosophy of respect to Law. I am not referring to Prohibition. This false philosophy of respect to law was being taught before Prohibition. Respect for law required people to return runaway slaves and permit wife whipping. This law, being a product of man's mind, it is like respecting *nafs* (ego). There is no principle. And when you add to it, the voluntary idea having people vote and change laws — there is no rock foundation to government.

America is a peculiar country which was founded on the principles of life, liberty and happiness. In that it is almost unique and approaches a providential government, only it has left no room for the providential person. So the Voice of God has not been heard in the land. Until this Voice of God is heard in the land there will be radical change in your institutions. Change is necessary and desirable but controlled change must come or chaos will result.

This is not a matter of evolution or revolution. Providence has nothing to do with that. Much of what is called evolution is hardly worthy of the name "change"; it had better be called drift. A directed revolution may be the salvation of any country, and undirected evolution leads nowhere. What is required, however, is not evolutionary or revolutionary change, but directed change.

GRACE
1939

On the fifteenth day of September, after I had pondered and meditated over the dream of the preceding day, the Voice of Silence came to me and said:

"Sufi Inayat Khan, in his day, had to abandon the arts for the hearts. Blessed are those arts which open the hearts and woe when the hearts are sacrificed for the arts. It has always been so, it will continue to be so. I would the hearts would rejoice of themselves not from any impressions that are forced upon them but of the light which comes from within. One mystical experience is worth a hundred even of sacred worldly treasures."

"THE NATIONS — THE PEOPLE"

Dec. 31, 1944

The nations! Lord, what of the nations?
"I made the people, not the nations,
It is the people who have created the nations.
Why not ask,'The people, what of the people?'
This people is Me, of My sinews and essence
I am the life in them and there is not else.
What are these boundary lines of which there is
    much to-do:
It is not I that marked the lines of severation,
It is not I who declared: 'This is one race, that is
    another',
It is not I who stirred those against these, these
    against those.
Who is there who looks for brotherhood!
It is they who have seen the blood of the dead and of
    the dying
It is they who know the sweet-delirium of
    all-suffering
The stay-at-homes are still in their stirrings,
The far-from-the-battle-line are ever active in their
    agitations,
So the world has no hope, continues in sorrow,
Continues in abomination, continues in tribulation
Where is Buddha? Where is Christ? Where is
    Moses?
Not in the hearts of worshippers who worship in
    blindness,

But in the awakened hearts — they are the Buddhas, the Moseses, the Christs.
But if the few accept not, how can the Nations?
Until the few enter the straight gate, the many shall remain at a loss.
They look to a Powerful Poland and care naught for the Poles!
They look for a renewed Hellas and turn their guns on the Greeks!
They look for the Land of Promise and shut the doors on the Jews!
And the Jews returning to their homeland shut the doors upon God.
Until God is put first, beware that man is not put last."

"EVEN THIS SMALL STEP"

March 2, 1945

Saith the Lord:
The men look to a meeting,
The people look to a greeting.
The delegates look to a seating,*
But where will the hearts look?
Oh peace, where art thou when races are divided!
Oh peace, what art thou when problems are hidden from view!

*The first U.N. meeting in San Francisco

264

But yet it is wonderful, wonderful that people even
    look one to another,
Wonderful, that even false efforts are to be made,
For out of the falseness will come the true,
Out of the hidden will arise the manifest.
When people sit down together to eat,
When people learn to enjoy mutual company,
When strangers come to appreciate the merits of
    one another,
Great steps are taken toward universal
    brotherhood.
Now the Hebrews call the Christians brethren
And the Christians for the most part reciprocate
But what are these brethren to me if they exclude
"Other sheep have I which are not of their folds."
Other sheep have I which do not compromise with
    material modernity.
Yet I recognize even this small step,
A blessing if indeed it is a step,
A curse if it be a finality.

"THE ARABS"

March 2, 1945

Lord, tell me of the Arabs, of the followers of the
    Prophet!
Then spaketh the Lord,
Out of the silence spake He.
My anger is kindled upon the persecutors.

Now they preach toleration.

Sometimes Muslims go to old mosques only

Sometimes Muslims are permitted to build or renew,

But to the money lender the poor are given full access.

Freedom always to borrow and pay forbidden usury.

So the poor are ground down even in the midst of prosperity,

While in adversity they fare still worse.

Therefore I say unto the children of men

If ye continue to grind the followers of the Prophet in usury

And Muslims if ye grind anybody in usury

Not all prayers shall hinder Hell-fire

Verily usury leadeth to Hell-fire even on earth.

If ye would return to Me, people of the Book,

Grant freedom and equality to the Muslims

Let their governments be of their own free choice.

And let them make mistakes even as ye permit one

Another not only to err but even to desecrate My Holy Laws.

"THE VISION OF THE ABODE FOR ONE AND ALL"

1946

In this section, Murshid was channelling Meher Baba during a brief visit to Baba's Myrtle Beach center. In later years, Murshid indicated that the building of the "Abode for One and All" would be taken up by others, as well as followers of Meher Baba.

I

The time may come when considerably more land will be added to the Abode for the One-and-All but each step should be taken with the highest degree of perfection possible. When you make a practice of doing as I say, I can be with you, each and every one of you, because I am your very breath and heartbeat.

This Academy of the One-and-All will not only be for God and humanity but will also aim to give man knowledge of the One-and of the All. As Abu Bakr Siddiq said, I see Allah and Shay (thing) together. For convenience sake we speak of the One, the All, as if they were different, apart. The Muslims used to have their science which dealt with the One (Allah) and with the all from which latter we obtain the sciences of the present day.

But the study of the All includes the arts as well as the sciences. It is the discriminating mind of man that has divided Nature into compartments which do not exist in reality and has called studies by separate names such as chemistry, physics, geology. Then it specializes more and more and invents endocrinology, parapsychology, ichthyology, and more and more specialized branches which are branches of investigation, not branches of knowledge.

The intuitive approach is different. The lines between the different sciences, between the different arts, between the sciences and arts begin to disappear.

The knowledge of the psychic processes is gained intuitively rather than through the intellect. The intellect gives knowledge of names and forms as if these were external. Actually what is external? Nothing can be proved to be external. So when the artist is sent out to draw a landscape he is placing on a canvas his impressions of part of God's earth. To do this in a perfect manner, or even in a good manner, he must have some consciousness of the relation of God and himself, of creation and himself. For this, meditation is most important.

The true artist is not a camera or a mere recording instrument. What he needs to do here, is to get the feeling of the unity between himself and his subject matter, or object matter. Now Allah is the life in him and also the cohesive power in that subject matter.

II

The fact that God appears in man and as man does not alter the truth that God is God. The stars hold to their courses, the chemical elements do not necessarily face a social or metaphysical revolution and women will continue to bear children. But there can be a widening of attitude, feeling and understanding which comes when man is aware of the Presence.

From the standpoint of science there are the principles of conservation of matter and energy. From the standpoint of God there is a universal economy. This universal economy will not be an excuse for a philosophy, it will be the way of life.

Biologists have already recognized the "cycle of life" as they call it. Vegetation draws from the soil and from the air. Animals feed on vegetation. And when the animals die their decayed bodies go to the dust of the earth and this in turn feeds the vegetation. Besides this the animal bodies breathe out carbon dioxide gas which is the food of plants which exhale oxygen and this is used by the animals and man. Without going into more detail one can say that this universal economy has been recognized.

In addition to this there are vibrations which come from God which impregnate the atmosphere and permeate the atomic structure. Without this divine sustenance the earth-globe would fall apart. These spiritual emanations are stronger in some places than in others and give rise to the recognition of shrines and sacred places.

III

The Center, or the Abode for One and All will be established in a manner which will avoid some of the basic errors made by the Great Religions in the Past. Buddha gave out the three jewels of the Buddha, Dharma or doctrine, and Sangha or Brotherhood. When he left this world there was a division of his followers as to their nature. Then Christ came and emphasized the Church, which also is to say, the Brotherhood. What happened instead was that the Church was institutionalized and man was supposed to give up his individual existence for this Church.

Now the time is come to awaken. The true brotherhood or church (Ikhwa) or sangha is not composed of people with faith or trust or love, certainly not of those with any particular set of beliefs. To become a member of this brotherhood one must taste of love or death or union with God, for the sake of God.

At the Center we are not going to be concerned with any theory of enlightenment. Whether it is Karma yoga or Bhakti yoga or even Jnana yoga does not matter.

Usually the tasks assigned will be of two natures. The Avatar may select the proficient so that the best work will be done with and through them as instruments. Or again, people will be selected for duties in order that samskaras may be removed and their egos liberated. But even in this work no one will be called to sacrifice for any institution called

Church or Brotherhood or Center or Ashram. The Abode-for-One-and-All is not separate from the One, nor separate from any individual of the All. The humanity belong to the Center and to the Master as the limbs and the organs and cells belong to the body, all are unseparate.

Neither is our work confined to certain planes. Clearing land may be an operation on a certain plane. Cleansing minds is an operation on another plane. As you do, God does. If you alone did, there would be no selfless service even with the best of intentions. Love could so easily be tainted with pride or conceit. It is even more important to get rid of pride and conceit. Love is natural to the soul.

So get rid of all snakes. It is the same thing. The poisonous snakes thrive because man is evil or does evil; the beneficial snakes prosper because man is good, does good. In any case snakes symbolize selfishness. The *Kadesh* of the Bible, the *Naga* of the Veda represent self-action. The snake's movement, the coiled spring, is symbolic of egocentricity. This is the source of all the world's evils. So I say get rid of all snakes, good or bad, *outer or inner*. Be like Saint Patrick.

Now you can see that the riddance of snakes, the clearing of brush and the removal of samskaras is one and the same process. I say remove all brush that will hide or protect animals, wild beasts. That is your physical dharma . . .

Conversely, landscape. Make beautiful curved paths. Lay out sites for artists' homes. This is the scope given to buddhic mind as the samskaras of the lower citta are removed. It is not all removal and destruction. It is building, it is construction, it is creation, it is beauty. It is the bestowal of grace and baka which accompanies or follows fana. It does not stop with neti, neti. After LA ILLAHA comes EL IL ALLAH. The negation of ego mind produces the affirmation of God.

Only be warned against too much zeal, against steps taken out of turn, against private interpretations of God's directions, against mental reflection and pleasure . . . in other words, against self coming under an apparent guise of selflessness.

My plans if you want to call them that for Lama definitely depend upon the acceptance that infants and little children are the mouthpieces of eternity. It is only after such acceptance that I can possibly present my personality. *—Letter to Lama   February 11, 1970*

AFTERWORD

Sam was one of the few people who have come to Lama, whether as teacher, staff or student, who understood what we have been attempting to manifest here. In his being he had realized what we had, until then, only conceptualized — a new awareness born of a planetary consciousness of the whole of humanity as a single family united in God.

This consciousness attested to increasingly by various masters from the nineteenth century onward was confirmed in our time as we watched the TV relays of the Apollo Mission, where for the first time we watched the earth as it rose above the rim of the moon and witnessed the dawn of a new age, a time in which it is no longer possible to deny the reality of our commonality; a time in which, one way or another, we will realize the meaning of "we are all one."

That moment sealed forever what was until then only a prophetic message. A message which begins: "Beloved Ones of God, you may belong to any race, caste, creed or nation, you are all impartially beloved by God." This message of spiritual unity has become manifest in an age when no place is beyond a day's journey. It has become necessary to acknowledge our unity as it is no longer possible to continue the fiction of the borders, be they national, cultural, or religious. Sectarianism and separatism vanish before the reality that the entire earth is our common heritage and that all contained within it and upon it was gifted to us and through us, and that we stand as stewards of this trust and inheritance which is ours through no doing on our part. Which is to say that there is none among us who has created the sun or moon or stars, none who has fashioned the rivers and valleys, none capable of forming the kernel of wheat or the least flower, nor is there anyone who has sure knowledge of such things.

It is through the various traditions and messages received from the beginning by all peoples, for there is no people to whom a messenger has not been sent, that we learn how it is "to be" in accord with our position as stewards of this trust, and it is in this way that we have invited various teachers to come to share with us the unique and discreet essence contained in their tradition, so that we might realize the truth contained in each, the better to fulfill both our karma and dharma as those born in the age of unity. SAM was the one who showed us the way in which to contain the ways, for he had applied himself and effaced himself into each until within his very being was a living knowledge of how the many are contained in the one. Through example he dissolved the paradoxes which arise from the horizontal perspective, why some say G-D while others say God, why some sit while others kneel and some dance while others pray. He showed us that there were not "ways" but "A" way and that way was exactly where we are at this very moment and moreover everything we need to tread that way is with us in this same moment. Through the vertical perspective which reveals the interlinked quality of all manifestation he pointed us toward the one, the source of all the "ways" which are like the rainbow rays of the pure lite after it has passed from its undifferentiated state through the mirrored prism of existentiation. We saw how each one was discreet and perfect; unique and beautiful; and how green was not red, nor was violet yellow, nor was Lord Buddha Jesus the Christ, nor Krishna Mohammed (Peace be upon them all). He taught us the wisdom of the heart which enabled us to love and honor each of the masters, saints and prophets, for they are all divine wisdom itself, appearing in different forms and names; all of whom are worthy of our love as the lover loves the beloved in all her different garments.

Through this teaching we realized the unity dwelling in the heart of the ways and traditions; he further showed to us the essence of that unity contained in the secrets of sound, the mysteries of the breath, the mantric reality of the divine logos and the holy word and flaming name that fills the void, that opens the door of the heart where there is no you or me but only this radiant suchness, this pure being, undivided and eternal.

Thought, conceptualization, intellectualizing are useful tools up to a point; beyond which it is necessary to say the WORD, dance the DANCE, manifest and materialize the secret in order that the word may become flesh, to know the Name in order to be known, to realize the self and so to become what it is that "I AM" is. With this awareness SAM set us to dancing and singing, the Raslila, the Divine Dance; each of us in contact with each other, left foot right foot, Allah-Allah-Allah, gathering us together, forming the circle, the living mandala, the Word in time with our movements. Through the Name, through our connection, through our breath and through our movement again and again we came together in the experience and reality of our essential unity. We are the circle of beings revolving in time to the ancient tune, the forgotten tune re-membered, put together and made whole, joined and merged as in the flow of faces we see the shadows of our forgotten ancestors as they turned and spun as we turn and spin; tracing the patterns of the desert geometry across the sands of time, turning and spinning until the Name becomes light and light, merging into breath, merges and emerges one out of the other as the breath that breathes; breathes us in and out, rising and falling, gone beyond-beyond-beyond. And always returning-returning into the world of sinks and dishes, breakfast and dinner, floors to sweep and windows to clean, wood to chop and water to haul, changing the baby and greasing the car; the ten million things that have to be done but no longer wondering who we are and what to do. Doing it all, all in the Name, every action each the same, breathing in and breathing out. It's all the dance, one foot in front of the other, ending as we begin in the Name of the One who is mercy and compassion.

Dusty Roads
Nakujabad, Spring 1975

GOD CALLS

The bells ring in the
   temple;
The perfume rises
   from the aloes;
The sage in
   meditation sits.
Om! Tat! Sat!
The nothingness
   of the now;
The Everythingness of Eternity.
God calls.

God calls.
The muezzin's voice from minaret tower
   cries:
"Come to prayer, come to prayer, come to
   prayer."
A million Moslems then stretch out their
   prayer rugs,
A million and a myriad million more.
"There is no God but God,

To this I now bear witness,
There is no God but God;
Mohammed is His Prophet; come to prayer."
God calls.

God calls.
On Friday eve the Jew prepares himself,
Walks to his synagogue and prays,
Takes down the Torah scroll and reads,
Reads what his forefathers read:
"Hear O Israel! The Lord our God, the Lord
    is One!"
"And His Name is One."
This is the Law and the prophets.
God calls.

God calls.
The stations slowly passing one by one,
She tells her beads and tells them o'er and
    o'er.
Ave Maria! Gratia plena!
Ora! Ora pro nobis!
Paternoster qui est in caelis,
Sanctificetur tuo nomen —
Sanctificetur! Sanctificetur!
God calls.

God calls.
The branches rustle lightly in the breeze,
Above the music of pagoda's bells.
His humble repeat finished ere 'tis noon,
The bhikshu tells the children of the
    Buddha,
They listen, one voice speaks in the forest,
Then all is silent, save the breeze . . . . .
There slowly comes that feeling of great
    peace.
Shanti! . . . Shanti! . . . Shanti! . . .
God calls.

God calls.
The men from every race have come
    together,
From every land, from every sect or cult.
They gather at the temple for their worship.
Love ye, every man his neighbor;
Be ye brethren, ye who are my brothers.
Worship Him, the Father of us all;
Worship Him, in Love and Faith and Joy;
Worship Him in Silence . . .
God calls.

Samuel L. Lewis (1927)

GLOSSARY

(Ar) - Arabic   (Ch) - Chinese   (Heb) - Hebrew
     (Jap) - Japanese   (Skr) - Sanskrit

abidharma – rules of right conduct (Skr)
Ain Soph – original wisdom-light (Heb)
akash – etheric element (Skr)
akhlak Allah – practicing the presence of God (Ar)
Allah ho akbar – "There is no power or might save in God";
   "Peace is power" (Ar)
ani, ani – I am (Heb)
Arya Dharma – Hinduism (Skr)
as salaam aleikum – "Peace be with you" (Ar)
asura – titan, demon, or jealous god; one of the realms in
   Hindu and Buddhist cosmology (Skr)
Avalokitashvara – the all-seeing Buddha of Compassion (Skr)
avatamsaka – principal scripture of Kegon school of
   Buddhism, emphasizing Oneness (rather than Emptiness)
   (Skr)
Avatar – Awakener; e.g., Rama, Krishna, Buddha, Christ
   (Skr)
avichi – one of the hell-realms in Hindu and Buddhist
   cosmology (Skr)
Baal Shem Tov – Speaker of the Good Name; founder of
   Hassidism (Heb)
baka – resurrection (after "fana", dissolution) (Ar)
baraka – blessing, grace (Ar)
bayat – spiritual initiation (Ar)
bhakti yoga – union in devotion (Skr)
Bhagavad Gita – "Song of God"; the central part of the
   Mahabharata, the story of Krishna (Skr)
Bismillah – "In the Name of God" (Ar)
bodhisattva – enlightened, selfless servant of humanity (Skr)
Chassidim (Hassidim) – followers of the Baal Shem Tov, Jews
   often compared to the Sufi dervishes (Heb)

Chisti – a Sufi order in India using music and dance
citta (chitta) – mind-stuff (Skr)
darood – mental repetition of "Toward the One" (Ar)
darshan – an interview; seeing a Master (Skr)
dayana (dhyana) – meditation (Skr)
dervish (darvish) – a God-intoxicated man; a Sufi (Ar)
dharma – the Way; righteous duty (Skr)
dharmakaya – formless, perfect body (Skr)
diksha – Hindu initiation (Skr)
fana – effacement of ego; dissolution of personality (Ar)
fana-fi-Lillah – effacement into God (Ar)
fana-fi-Rassoul – effacement into the Messenger of God (Ar)
fikar (fikr) – Remembrance of God, mental Zikr (Ar)
fudo — Protector of the Dharma (Jap)
gatha – song; scripture (Skr)
Gautama – Nepalese prince who became Shakyamuni Buddha
    (Skr)
gina – Buddha; the Victorious One (Skr)
gita – scripture; song (Skr)
gopi – the female devotee who dances in ecstasy to the sound
    of Krishna's flute (Skr)
guru – spiritual guide; the ideal in human form (Skr)
hal – ecstasy (Ar)
hara – energy center below and behind navel (Jap)
hare – hail, praise to (Skr)
Ikhwa (Ikhwan) – Brotherhood (Ar)
jai – fulfillment, victory (Skr)
jhanas – meditative breathing practices given by Lord
    Buddha (Skr)
jnana yoga (gyan yoga) – way of knowledge or intellect (Skr)
Kadesh – Jewish prayer for the soul of the dead (Heb)
kalama – call of God (Ar)
karma – law of cause and effect (Skr)
karma yoga – union in action; selfless service (Skr)
karuna – compassion (Skr)
kashf – insight (Ar)
khalif – representative of a Pir or Murshid (Ar)
khanka – a Sufi gathering place (Ar)

khilvat – Sufi hermitage or retreat (Ar)

khirka – cloak, or mantle (Ar)

Khizr (Kwaja Khidr) – the "green man"; an aspect of Gabriel; Elijah (Ar)

koan – Zen riddle, a meditative exercise designed to awaken (Jap)

Krishna – God of Love (Skr)

Kung-tse (Kung-fu-tse) – Confucius (Ch)

kurukshetra – the final battle (in the Bhagavad Gita) (Skr)

La illaha el Allah Hu (or, La illaha illa' 'llah) — "There is naught — but God"; the central affirmation of the Muslim and the Sufi (Ar)

mahamudra – Mahayana Buddhist meditation; "the Great Gesture" (Skr)

mahayana – "the Great Vehicle"; applied to Tibetan and Zen Buddhism as well as others (Skr)

Maitreya – the coming Buddha; Buddha of Compassion (Skr)

manas – lower mind (Skr)

Manjusri – Buddha of skillful means (Skr)

mantra – sacred phrase; use of the science of sound in sacred phrase (Skr)

manusha – mental realm (Skr)

maya – the world of phenomena; illusion (Skr)

moksha – liberation (Skr)

muezzin – Muslim leader of prayer (Ar)

mujahida – "greater holy war" (with the enemies within one's self) (Ar)

murakkaba – concentration; meditation (Ar)

mureed – Sufi disciple (Ar)

Murshid – Sufi Master; spiritual teacher (Ar)

nafs – personality complex (Ar)

naga – mythic snake (Skr)

Nakshibandi – a Sufi order; symbology (Ar)

Namo Amida Butsu – "Hail to the Buddha of the Western Paradise" (Jap)

naraca – personification of a subhuman state in Hindu and Buddhist cosmology (Skr)

Nayaz – Sufi healing prayer (Ar)

neti, neti – Hindu way of negation; "not this, not that" (Skr)

Nirguna Brahma – formless God (Skr)

nirmanakaya – manifest realm (Skr)

nirvana – the unconditioned state; beyond beyond (Skr)

nufsaniat – world of phenomena (Ar)

passim – various writings of (Lat.)

Pir – head of a Sufi order (Ar)

prajna – wisdom; insight (Skr)

prakriti – Nature; the Mother (Skr)

prana – spirit breath; energy (Skr)

pranavada – knowledge of the science of breath (Skr)

pranayama – science and control of prana or breath (Skr)

purusha – spirit, in contrast to prakriti (Skr)

qwali – Sufi singer (Ar)

rakshasa – the animalic beings in Hindu and Buddhist cosmology (Skr)

Ram – hero of the solar dynasty; also identified with the unmanifest God (Skr)

raslila – the dance or play of God (Krishna) (Skr)

Rassoul – Messenger; Avatar (Ar)

roshi – Zen Master (Jap)

ryazat – esoteric teaching (Ar)

Sadguru – true, perfect Guide (Skr)

Sakyamuni – the last incarnate Buddha (Gautama) (Skr)

sambogakaya – creative, archetypal world; rainbow realm (Skr)

sama – Sufi gathering to hear holy music (Ar)

samadhi – highest stages of meditation; experience of unity (Skr)

samkhya – yoga philosophy (Skr)

samskara – impressions resulting from actions (Skr)

sangha – (Buddhist) Brotherhood (Skr)

satori – realization (Jap)

shafayat – healing (Ar)

Shankaracharya – incarnation of Shiva; the first sannyasi, and founder of the Swami Order (Skr)

sannyasi – mendicant who has taken vows (Skr)

shay – the individual thing (Ar)

sheikh – Sufi or Muslim teacher or leader of community (Ar)
shekina – indwelling spirit (Heb)
Shiva – God of destruction or of transformation (Skr)
Shiva/Shakti – spirit/power (Skr)
shuvo – turning one's face to God; repentance (Heb)
sifat – attributes (Ar)
sifat-i-Allah – the ninety-nine attributes of God (Ar)
sramana – wandering monk; ascetic (Skr)
sukhavati – paradise of bliss (Skr)
sukr – state of intoxication (Ar)
sutra – scriptural verse (Skr)
Sufi – (variously) from "Sophia," the Wise, "Saf," the Pure, or "suf," wool, origin uncertain
tantra – conscious transformation of energy; often misrepresented in the West (Skr)
tasbih – Sufi or Muslim rosary (prayer beads) (Ar)
tassawuf – Sufism (Ar)
Tassawuri – attunement to a Master (Ar)
tathagata – suchness; essence; the name given to Sakyamuni Buddha after his enlightenment (Skr)
tatwamasi – "that thou art" (Skr)
tauba – turning toward God; repentance (Ar)
upanishads – the 108 closing books of the Vedas (Skr)
Vedas – ancient Hindu scriptures (Skr)
volvox – a genus of waterborne, spherical organisms (Lat.)
wasifa – (see sifat-i-Allah) divine attributes often repeated orally (Ar)
yoga – "union"; the practice of coming to God (Skr)
Zen – Japanese Buddhism descended from Chan Buddhism of China (Jap)
zendo – Zen meditation hall (Jap)
zikar (zikr) – Remembrance of God; repetition of the phrase, "La illaha illa' 'llah" — "There is no god but God; none exists save He" (Ar)
zat – essence (Ar)

BIBLIOGRAPHY - S.A.M.'S
SUGGESTIONS FOR FURTHER READING

(From "Vision and Ritual in Sufism" and "Genuine Mystical Experience")

Aurobindo, Sri	*The Life Divine*
Arberry, A.J.	*The Discourses of Rumi*
	Muslim Saints & Mystics
	Translation of Farid-ed-din Al Attar
Brown J.P.	*The Dervishes*
Browne, E.G.	*History of Persian Literature*
	A Year Among the Persians
Brunton, Paul	Passim
Burckhardt, Titus	Passim
Das, Swami Ram	Passim
Hafiz	Passim
Hujwiri, Al	*Kashf-al-Mahjub (Trans: Nicholson)*
Khan, Hazrat Inayat	*Passim, published and unpublished*
	The Sufi Message (12 volumes)
Unknown	*Irfan* (privately published)
Lings, Martin	*A Muslim Saint of the Twentieth Century*
Muller, Max	*Passim*
Nasr, Seyyed Hossein	*Three Muslim Sages* (Also: Sufi Essays)
Quran	Many versions
Rehatsek	*The Gulisant of Sa'di*
Radakrishna, Sarvepalli	Passim
Sasaki, Ruth	Passim
Sasaki, Sokei An	*The Cat's Yawn*
Senzaki, Nyogen	Passim, Published and unpublished
Shah, Idries	*The Sufis* and Passim

Al-Surhawardi, Abdullah	*The Sayings of Muhammed*
	L'awarifu. Ma'Arif
Sharib, Z.H.	*Khawaja Gharib Nawaz (The Life of Moineddin Chisti)* pub. by Sheikh M.
M. Ashraf	
Tabriz, Shams-i-	*The Whirling Ecstasy*
Udman, Fuard	*Ishq-u-Wa Qalb*

PUBLISHED WORKS
OF MURSHID SAMUEL LEWIS

From Prophecy Pressworks:
  Introduction to Spiritual Dance
  The Jerusalem Trilogy
  The Rejected Avatar
  Toward Spiritual Brotherhood
  Introduction to Spiritual Dance and Walk, Vols. 1 & 2
From Sufi Community Press (formerly Ikhwan Press):
  Crescent and Heart
  Spiritual Walk
  Suras of the New Age
From Omen Press:
  This is the New Age in Person

All available through Rainbow Bridge Distributing Co., P.O. Box 40208, San Francisco, CA 94114.

For further information concerning the above publications or the spiritual practices referred to in this book, contact Sufi Islamia Ruhaniat Society, 410 Precita Avenue, San Francisco, CA 94110.

khatum

O Thou, Who art the Perfection
   of Love, Harmony, and Beauty,
The Lord of heaven and earth,
Open our hearts, that we may
   hear Thy voice,
Which constantly cometh from within.
Disclose to us Thy Divine Light,
Which is hidden in our souls,
That we may know and understand
   life better.
Most Merciful and Compassionate God,
Give us Thy great Goodness;
   Teach us Thy loving Forgiveness;
Raise us above the distinctions and
   differences which divide us.
Send us the Peace of Thy Divine Spirit,
And unite us all in Thy Perfect Being.

                                         Amen